I0074064

THE CHASE CONTINUES

ARMINLEAR

The Chase Continues
Copyright © 2022 by Charles A. Lowenhaupt
All rights reserved under the Pan-American and International Copyright
Conventions. This book may not be reproduced in whole or in part, except for
brief quotations embodied in critical articles or reviews, in any form or by any
means, electronic or mechanical, including photocopying, recording, or by any
information storage and retrieval system now known or hereinafter invented,
without written permission of the publisher, Armin Lear Press.

Library of Congress Control Number: 2022946295

ISBN (hardback): 978-1-956450-44-6
(paperback): 978-1-956450-45-3
(eBook): 978-1-956450-46-0

Armin Lear Press Inc
215 W Riverside Drive, #4362
Estes Park, CO 80517

THE CHASE CONTINUES

FREEDOM FROM WEALTH AS YOU AGE

CHARLES A. LOWENHAUPT

ARMINLEAR

CONTENTS

PREFACE

It has been ten years since Don Trone and I wrote *Freedom from Wealth: The Experience and Strategies to Help Protect and Grow Private Wealth*; and it has been four years since I completed *The Wise Inheritor's Guide to Freedom from Wealth: Making Family Wealth Work for You*. Over that period, I have progressed from middle age to old age, and I have watched my clients and friends get older as well. And in that time, many began approaching me, pointing out that they had passed that state of "inheritor" and youth and asking me what advice I could provide now that they'd entered their "golden years."

In considering how to "continue the chase"—following your dreams and achieving self-actualization—throughout old age, and despite its challenges, in addition to my own experience, I fortunately have the experience of those same clients and friends to draw on. You will notice that, throughout this book, most of my models for what works—and what doesn't—come from my parents, grandparents, and clients. All come from "real life," and I share their stories to help you on your journey.

People also often ask me when they should start thinking about how to handle the many obstacles and opportunities that arise with old age. Inevitably, my answer is the sooner the better. Thinking strategically gets harder as you get older, whether considering your own circumstances or those of others. You may be thinking about how to continue the chase for yourself, or you may be thinking about how to help others—parents, clients, those for whom you feel some responsibility—fulfill their dreams. In every case, starting now is not likely too soon.

If you have read my earlier books, you will already know the process I recommend to ensure your own self-actualization in youth. If you have not read my books, or never considered self-actualization before, that's quite alright. Many wealthy adults reach middle age so consumed with earning a living, raising children, or struggling with life's challenges, they have never stopped to consider how they want to become all they can be. You might not yet have a chase you want to continue. But in that void, you have an exciting and challenging opportunity to decide what dream you want to chase, what person you want to be. Wherever you are in the chase—at the starting line or within sight of the finish line—get on with it.

You may be contemplating your own future or the future of your loved ones or others you care for. I hope this volume helps you accept old age and consider the strategies to enjoy it with the same purpose and freedom from the burdens of wealth available at every stage of life. In other words, I hope this book gives you the tools to self-actualize regardless of your age.

ACKNOWLEDGMENTS

As I have considered how to continue the chase throughout old age and despite its many challenges, in addition to my own experience, I have had the experiences of my friends and family to draw on. You will notice that, throughout this book, most of my models for what works—and what doesn't—come from my parents, grandparents, and clients. I acknowledge their love and friendship with my thanks and affection.

I also acknowledge with gratitude the support and advice I have received as I wrote this book from my editor, Zach Gajewski, and my advisor, Greg Berardi. Among those whose support I have especially relied on throughout my work on this book, I include my business partners, Carolyn Ohlsen and Chris Quinn, and all my colleagues at Lowenhaupt & Chasnoff and Lowenhaupt Global Advisors. Bringing this book into the world also required the help of my accomplished publisher, Maryann Karinch.

Always by my side, through youth and age, is my wife—who never seems to reach old age—whose love has supported me for more than fifty years. She tolerates my old age and always allows me to continue the chase. My acknowledgments would not be complete without including my daughters, their husbands and my grandchildren, all of whom give me both the perspective needed to accept I have reached old age and their love.

INTRODUCTION

Amid utter want old age cannot be a light thing, not even to a wise man; nor to a fool, even amid utmost wealth, can it be otherwise than burdensome.
– Cicero, "Cato Maior de Senectute"

In 44 BC, a year before he died, the Roman philosopher, scholar, and statesman Marcus Tullius Cicero penned the "Cato Maior de Senectute." His essay on aging and death spoke to a universal truth: without financial security, getting older can certainly be difficult, but wealth in itself does not guarantee comfort, ease, and carefree twilight years either. For those who have been fortunate enough to create or inherit substantial wealth in their lifetimes, this statement may come as a shock. Many believe the accumulation of wealth over the years—or in one lucky fell swoop—should be enough to live life to the fullest in their sixties, seventies, eighties, and beyond. But time and time again, this belief has been proven wrong. No matter the source or timing of the wealth, enjoying old age requires more than the right financial investments.

Cicero reflects on an ideal image of old age when he points to the statesman Appius:

> *Appius, though he was both blind and old, managed four sturdy sons, five daughters, a great household, and many dependents; for he did not languidly succumb to old age, but kept his mind ever taut, like a well-strung bow. He maintained not mere authority, but absolute command over his household . . . his children revered him, all loved him, and the customs and discipline of his forefathers flourished beneath his roof.[1]*

Appius had mental acuity and loving children and household. He maintained control over himself, his decisions, and his home—an ability that allowed him to grow old happily. And his legacy carries on today, as he is remembered centuries later for building Rome's first road and first aqueduct and is seen as one of Rome's earliest literary figures.

But you need not have been a famous statesman and author to have secured a lasting legacy in Roman times. Just as Cicero tells us of Appius's accomplishments, he also describes unnamed Roman farmers.

> *But come now—to pass over these divine pursuits—I can point out to you Roman farmers in the Sabine country, friends and neighbors of mine, who are scarcely ever absent from the field while the more important operations of husbandry, as sowing, reaping, and storing the crops, are going on. Although this interest of theirs is less remarkable in the case of annual crops—for no one is so old as to think that he cannot live one more year—yet these same men labor at things which they know will not profit them in the least.*

He plants the trees to serve another age, as our
Caecilius Statius says in his Young Comrades. And if
you ask a farmer, however old, for whom he is planting,
he will unhesitatingly reply, "For the immortal gods,
who have willed not only that I should receive these
blessings from my ancestors, but also that I should hand
them on to posterity."

The old farmer's vision continues through old age, preserving blessings for future generations. He pursues a plan, not just for himself, but for those who will come after him.

Cicero's thinking about old age as he looks at Appius or his neighboring farmers is not likely to be substantially different from our own. Think about it: If asked "What do you want in old age?" your answer is likely to include one or more of the answers suggested by Cicero. Indeed, consider one, or more, of the following:

- Good health
- Independence
- Continued strength
- Activity and pursuit of interests
- Family
- Safety
- Control
- A continuing mission and legacy
- And "influence" (the crowning glory of old age, as Cicero called it)

Picture an elderly Sir Winston Churchill, cigar in his mouth, easel set up and brush in hand, enjoying the liberties of life without the responsibilities of governance. Churchill was often photographed in this exact way later in life. The image embodies nearly all of these visions—he's a man at peace, in charge of himself and doing something he loves. He has a legacy as a historian, a politician, and a warrior. He has maintained his well-known vigor and independence, and the look on his face reflects a sense of contentment and joy.

Unfortunately, many wealth holders enter their final years without a vision or a plan. Most of us are so busy leading life in our thirties, forties, and fifties, we don't think or prepare for our sixties and beyond. This aimless approach to aging leaves many of us without the contentment enjoyed by Appius, the farmer, or Churchill.

Though Cicero provided great wisdom on aging two millennia ago, his advice has been lost on many of us today. And, of course, times have changed. Modern living has only complicated the situation. Cicero reminds us that aging well is a battle: "For old age is honored only on condition that it defends itself, maintains its rights, is subservient to no one, and to the last breath rules over its own domain." As a wealth holder in the twenty-first century, you cannot blindly enter this battle—you need a plan.

A BATTLE PLAN FOR OLD AGE

As a ninety-five-year-old gentleman who created a large and prosperous business once said to me, "In its final chapters, life can be most fulfilling. Your dreams are realized, and you can take comfort in having passed on a positive legacy to your successors. But it is often a struggle to help them. Contentment in old age is the deliberate result of dreaming when you are young and realizing those dreams. The truth is that growing old is not easy." This man knew that well-being in old age requires a vision about the future, even when it seems distant. You need to be prepared, set priorities, and build strategies to accomplish them. You cannot wait until the first cannon fires to join the fight.

Planning for old age must be comprehensive, going far beyond living wills, final directives, up-to-date "estate planning," or the various "products" often sold to the aging. It must include scenario planning and candid conversations with people on whom you will rely. In my family's work with individuals and families of significant wealth, the problem we have seen over and over is that many start planning *too late in life*. When old age has arrived, the prospect of aging well has already begun to slip away.

For more than 100 years, my family's law firm, Lowenhaupt & Chasnoff, has helped countless high net-worth clients manage their wealth, including six generations in one family. Founded in 1908 by my grandfather—the first attorney concentrating in the federal income tax—our firm has worked with individuals and families of significant wealth to develop a coherent and workable vision of old age. Whatever the vision—whether family harmony, independence, financial safety, or just waking up every morning looking forward to the day—it takes planning. And this planning must start years *before* old age sets in, when a person can still think clearly and objectively. What seems obvious to a sixty-year-old may seem preposterous to a ninety-year-old.

Because dementia and confusion are likely to hit most of us some day the plan needs to soften any descent as your mental faculties diminish. Your plan should allow you to rely on others you trust, rather than trying to exercise capabilities you no longer have. Those caring for you must know and respect your thoughts, feelings, and plans, and they need to embrace your desires about growing old.

And, like Cicero's farmer, your plan must allow you to pass on the legacy and wisdom as you see fit, planting the trees that will grow tall for future generations.

In many ways, developing this plan is part of a lifetime pursuit, an answer to the question you must ask regardless of age. Long before you get lost in the weeds of planning, this fundamental question must be carefully addressed: What is your wealth for? The answer to that question is rarely "to keep me busy trying to master my finances and count my gold like King Midas." Likewise, the answer is never "to preserve" or "to enhance" wealth. Wealth is preserved or enhanced to achieve its intended purpose.

So, what is the answer?

THE FREEDOM TO LIVE FULLY

After a lifetime of work, the answer appears obvious to me. It wasn't, however, for a gentleman who came to my office one day. Over the years, he had turned a small investment into $1 billion. When I asked him why he had come to see us, he replied he wanted to reduce his income and estate taxes. Certainly, we could help him in that regard; we had been doing that for decades, ever since my grandfather created the new discipline of income tax law. But then I said, "You've told me what your wealth is *not* for—you don't want to pay taxes. I want to know what your wealth is for."

After a considerable pause he asked, "What are my choices?"

I truly believe the purpose of your wealth is *self-actualization*—the realization and fulfillment of your greatest self. In other words, wealth should help you become all you can be. Each person will define that differently but living life to its fullest is the ultimate goal. Without a fundamental understanding of the purposes of wealth, there can be no satisfaction, regardless of your age. If when you are young you don't create a plan to live a fulfilling life, wealth can become a burden, especially as you age. You must therefore discover who you are and what you want out of life.

Self-actualization is an ongoing challenge, a work in progress, and wealth can surprisingly make it more difficult to achieve if it is not put in its proper place. That's why I have long been a proponent of what I refer to as "freedom from wealth." Freedom from wealth does not mean you cast aside your financial fortune. Rather, you use wealth to expand your opportunities, not limit them. I examined this topic in my first book, *Freedom from Wealth*. I also analyzed it from another vantage point in *The Wise Inheritor's Guide To Freedom from Wealth*, which focused on how wealth inheritors can become all they can be.

In the course of my work, I have found that aging—a topic no one likes discussing—hasn't been examined in the context of freedom from wealth. But if you have enjoyed freedom from wealth as a younger person, isn't it natural to live that way in your golden years? That's the purpose of this book: To help you achieve freedom from wealth and continue to self-actualize into old age.

CONTINUING THE CHASE

In his book, *Chasing the American Dream*, Washington University Professor Mark Rank, describes the universal human desire to have the freedom passionately to pursue self-actualization. He emphasizes that the pursuit is a journey. Importantly, it requires financial security, as well as optimism. In my previous books, I wrote at length about individuals who create enormous wealth by chasing their dream, but who then later mistakenly redefine their dream as having money. Too often, their initial dream fades into memory as they and their family become accustomed to wealth. They are left with no dream to chase.

So as wealth holders age, their greatest challenge becomes knowing how to continue the chase with vigor and optimism. In this book, we frequently refer to the chase and how aging can become an impediment to it. But the beginning of the journey really needs to start by defining the dream or dreams to be chased. The lucky ones conceive of that vision in their youth and pursue it into old age. Figuring out how to pursue the dream into old age can be a challenge and is one we will examine throughout this book. Failure to meet that challenge can make old age frustrating and unhappy.

A client and friend was a brilliant stockbroker. He understood every company he invested in by studying balance sheets, meeting with management, and actively engaging in the marketplace. He was also a great philanthropist, and a person as involved in his community as anyone I have ever met. He was incredibly active, serving on boards, in political activities, and as a volunteer. He had a great capacity to mentor younger people in community engagement. As a fifty-year old, he would have defined his "dream" as the old farmer would—he wanted to help young people "plant the trees" for future generations.

Well into his seventies, he continued building his fortune, as well as those of his clients, and serving his community. He worked alone, never able to maintain a working relationship with any of the young people he brought into his firm. Yet, these young people admired him and sought out his advice. And that advice, whether as a broker or a mentor, was priceless. Unfortunately, the ravages of age took their toll. He developed cancer and suffered for two years before he died. During those years, he found himself unable to keep up with his "companies" or even to maintain his own books. His clients left him.

Without succession in his business, he was overwhelmed and found no time at all for his community activities. Spending day in and day out at his office, desperately trying to maintain the business, he disappeared from sight. In his final months, he told his wife and me that his business was worthless. The portfolio had declined because he could not manage it. He warned his wife that she would be destitute after his death, and I believed him. (In fact, after his death, we found stocks and bonds he owned worth tens of millions of dollars.)

That broker was enslaved during the final years of his life. His oppressor was not so much the cancer as himself and the inability to manage his responsibilities to his clients and his family. Because he had no support, he constantly worried about his financial future. In fact, it was impossible to chase a dream because he believed he had no financial security. He missed the chance to benefit from the joy and sustenance that comes from helping others. That was no way to die.

Of course, it doesn't have to be this way. Optimism flows from the excitement of a executing a "mission" each day. Many veterans who return home from war still yearn for a daily mission. An illustrative example is the Veterans Organization, The Mission Continues. It helps returning members of the armed forces retain a clear sense of purpose after active military duty. It helps them find social service projects, such as school repair and maintenance, and working in underserved communities, in addition to other projects. For the aging wealth holder, a fulfilling mission could be focused on the community in social services or philanthropy. Then there's Cicero's farmer, who carried on the mission of his ancestors, planting trees that he saw as blessings that he had received and would pass on. A living, modern example is former President Jimmy Carter. Now in his nineties, every morning he wakes up to a mission to help the community. He tirelessly supports various charities, such as Habitat for Humanity, and serves as an emissary when asked.

The mission is usually an extension of activity during your life. The farmer of many years plants trees. Or the mission could be an entirely new pursuit that offers fresh challenges and rewards. Almost always, if the mission is rooted in community, it will yield positive results and recognition from others, which generates even more inspiration and optimism.

Aging should not stop your chase, nor does it have to, but your mission must be manageable as you age. That means thinking ahead about many of the things you currently take for granted: your health, home, mobility, transportation, work, leisure activities, partners and loved ones, and more. And when you can no longer manage all this, you will need assistance. That may take the form of support from a wide range of people, such as financial advisors, lawyers, accountants, doctors, geriatricians, social workers, and family.

Despite all of your wealth, without a plan, you will deprive yourself of the ability to chase your dream in old age. As a result, you may find yourself like many unprepared aging wealth holders: focused on infirmities, deluged with healthcare issues, or a sedentary contemplation of death. That's no way to live what should be the best years of your life.

STRATEGIES THAT DEFINE AGING ON YOUR TERMS

The chapters that follow articulate the strategies that will enable you to chase your dream and carry on your mission into old age. This work provides insights and stories about individuals who are living free from the burdens of wealth and are self-actualizing even in old age. Every person must define that mission and update it as warranted. To that end, each one of these chapters tackles a topic that will be universal to the success of your mission. Each of the chapters may appear to be its own challenge, but together, they are part of a larger goal of living life to its fullest.

This book also speaks to the many people you are likely to call upon—professionals, family members, and friends. These people will be involved in setting the relevant priorities and designing the necessary support system for you. They will give you—the aging wealth holder—a helping hand and will allow you to retain control of your life as your capabilities decline. Drawing on my experience working with families and with experts in aging, I describe a strategic approach to aging and all of the steps to create a workable plan for the wealth holder and his or her support network.

Now let's begin at the natural starting point for designing that plan for successful aging—setting priorities.

CHAPTER 1
PRIORITIES: SETTING THE STAGE TO CONTINUE YOUR CHASE

Twentieth-century German American psychologist Erik Erikson posited that people's psychosocial development takes place over eight stages during the course of their lives. As people enter Erikson's eighth, and final stage, they are expected to look back and consider whether they've been successful or unsuccessful. As they examine their pasts, they are expected to feel either pride in their accomplishments or regret over their failures. In effect, according to Erikson, this final stage of life is relatively passive and almost entirely contemplative—a stage of wisdom or depression.

My background and education do not qualify me to quibble with Erikson. However, many wealth holders age well and continue their chase, instead of sitting around and thinking about their past. Money and financial security make that chase easier (though they are rarely the object of a successful chase). For example, I've known Benedictine monks who have continued to study and teach well into their nineties. Financially comfortable, they do not need to provide for their food, laundry, housing, and basics, so they can devote their full energy to their activities.

Another example is a great collector I knew. He passionately studied, lectured, and wrote about rare coins, books, maps, and other historical objects. All three floors of his large house were stuffed with items from his collection, filling up each one of the offices he had on each floor. As he entered his seventies, he and his wife had an elevator installed to take him from floor to floor. The couple retained a full-time cook, laundress, housemaid, and driver. He continued writing books, giving lectures, and collecting objects well past his 100th birthday. He died with an active mind at age 103.

Still another illustrative example of a person who was able to continue chasing his dreams was a tax lawyer I knew. He moved from Boston to an easily accessible apartment in Southern California when he was ninety years old. There, he was near family who could help him with grocery shopping and medical care. He maintained a full team of household help and happily used taxicabs rather than drive himself. He continued to practice a bit of tax law, advising a few of his older clients, read tax literature, and followed every legislative development. He took great pride in the fact that he prepared his own tax returns every year. At age 106, after finishing up his returns, he walked them to the post office, and then came home, all on April 14. That night, when he died in his sleep, fully filed and compliant with the tax law, he had not known he would be saving his executor from the obligation to prepare his prior year's return.

These vibrant people lived successfully into old age, doing much more than simply reflecting back on life. Each enthusiastically continued his chase that had begun long before old age crept up on him. Each knew what he wanted out of life and had a sense of purpose as he continued to chase his dream. Those men set priorities and then planned for eventualities that might limit the fulfillment of those priorities. They did this by installing elevators, moving to apartments without stairs, or living in a monastery where food and laundry were seamlessly provided. All of them had the necessary financial support, so there were no financial constraints. As important, each had personal support—people who knew what would be needed and could ensure those needs were met.

Financial support and personal support are key, but neither helps you chase your dream unless you and your support network know what your dream is. Fundamentally, you need to start by setting your priorities and then planning for, and communicating, them. You must therefore consider what will be important to you as you age and what might interfere in the ongoing pursuit of your interests. You start by setting and analyzing priorities.

ANALYZING PRIORITIES

My ninety-year-old dentist was one of the best of his generation. His reputation for excellence was unparalleled. Dental schools throughout the country taught lessons based on his articles and books, and everyone in the field knew his name and had high regard for his reputation. I spent time living out of town in Boston, New York, and Ann Arbor where I went to other dentists. Each of them could take one look at my teeth and identify my dentist as the architect: "He is one of the greatest dentists in the U.S. and respected everywhere."

One day, I asked my dentist, "What happens when you are not here to take care of me?"

"Don't worry," he answered. "I will let you know when the time comes."

Not surprisingly, that time never came. Out of the blue, I received a letter purportedly from him, saying he had retired. Four months later, he called to ask me when I planned to come in for an appointment. "What about the letter?" I asked.

"My son wrote it—without my consent—to you and all my other patients," he said. "Pay no attention to it. I am in charge."

In fact, he was not in charge. He was unhappy—and I had already found another dentist. I heard many people say, "Poor old guy, he really lost it." Without having identified his priorities and making them clear to his son, he was unable to create a respectable transition of the business. As my dentist aged, he should have developed and shared that plan with his son, who could have then helped accomplish that transition. Unfortunately, that didn't happen, and it marred the relationships the dentist enjoyed with his patients, not to mention his professional reputation. An attitude like my dentist's—"I will let you know when the time comes"—rarely works. Instead, priorities need to be well defined and shared with family, friends, or advisors.

What would that dentist have wanted if he had been asked thirty years earlier? That's when he should have considered his priorities, expressed them, figured out how to implement them, and identified any possible impediments. Suppose my dentist had said his priority was maintaining his professional reputation. In that case, one of his strategies may have included continuing his writing even after he no longer could treat patients. Or if his priority was taking care of patients over the long term, strategies would have included the creation of a clear succession plan to transition patients during his retirement. In either case, his son could have assisted him. No matter the specific priorities, he should have protected himself against scenarios where they could be frustrated, such as his becoming ill—or losing sight—and thereby eliminating his ability to take care of patients or write or lecture.

So, priorities need to be set, strategies must be developed, and both need to be communicated to those who can help implement them. How the analysis is performed and completed—with whom the priorities are set—can be almost as important as the priorities themselves. Formalization of priorities can follow through trusts, living wills, declarations of desires, or personal constitutions. Then they all must be implemented and monitored through regular reconsideration. If you set those priorities yourself, they can still be perfectly valid, but without the engagement of those who will help you manage them, they can become lost in a haze of old age and lack of clarity. Potential obstacles may also be overlooked. Therefore, assistance from others is necessary to ensure your priorities are well defined and fully honored.

EXPLAINING YOUR PRIORITIES

Priorities need to be carefully crafted. They are, by nature, quite general, but discussion may be necessary to understand your specific intent. "Good health," for example, is often considered a priority with age, but that can be difficult to interpret. Is "good health" a condition that allows people to do what they want, while "bad health" keeps them from doing the same activities? At age thirty-five, waking up sore and stiff every morning might seem unbearable (and a sign of bad health), but by age seventy-five, those aches and pains may be perfectly acceptable. There are many elderly people who carry oxygen tanks around with them who would have "rather died than do that" when they were forty years younger. So, health needs to be defined in terms of how it can interfere with your priorities. Good health should not be defined the same by a seventy-year-old as a twenty-year-old.

Similarly, "independence" is a great priority, but in settling on that priority you should consider the tension between independence and safety. For example, if as you age, you're prone to falling or bouts of forgetfulness, living alone may no longer be a viable option. Still, you may be able to maintain a sense of independence that works for you by having a caretaker check in on you every day, a driver to take you to and from any appointments or social gatherings, and someone to prepare meals for you on a regular basis. Though you will likely miss getting behind the wheel or cooking your favorite dishes, by allowing someone else to take on those burdens, you retain your independence. This may not be the independence you enjoyed fresh out of college, but by defining independence as you get older, you'll be better able to pinpoint what you can do to make sure it stays intact.

To best define and rank your priorities, start by developing a list. That list can change over time, but writing down what's most important to your future happiness will create a clear picture of your top priorities. The list should be carefully ordered and modest in length. When you try to prioritize every aspect of life, you end up having no priorities at all. A priority list of five or six items may be manageable; twenty would be overwhelming. Once you've developed this list and thought it through, don't just leave it to collect dust. Instead, discuss it with those on whom you are likely to depend in your later years.

HONORING PRIORITIES

When my father died, my mother was in her early seventies. Within a year of his death, I sat down with her and asked her what her priorities were. I explained that, together, we could develop ways to achieve them. Generally, her independence was most important to her. She rarely considered illness as an obstacle so, surprisingly, her health was not on her list. Perhaps unrealistically, but very much in character, she said, "I am not worried about my health; it can take care of itself, and I will deal with whatever may come."

Her highest priority was to stay in the apartment she and my father had moved into many years before. No matter what, she did not want to leave that home. We discussed the fact that she might be lonely without the companionship a retirement home might provide; that she might need intrusive twenty-four-hour care for her safety; and that independent living could be expensive. After discussing all of these possibilities, she maintained that living at home was still her highest priority.

As for her second highest priority, it was that she could always have a male companion as long as she wanted. We noted that might mean she would end up supporting someone financially, or that he might be someone her children did not like. We also discussed the fact that she might have to care for him or arrange care for him. She recognized those possibilities and said she was willing to live with them. She then stated that her third priority was that she never would remarry.

We discussed these, and other, priorities, and then reviewed them annually. She survived my father by more than twenty years, living until age ninety-seven. Though she had diminishing executive function (and corresponding twenty-four-hour care) for the last ten years of her life, she never moved out of her apartment, she had two male companions (one at a time) up to her ninety-second year, and she never remarried.

Based on her clearly defined priorities, decisions were easy to make. For example, for a time, her second boyfriend lived with her, but as he became less competent with age, he unfortunately became more disruptive to my mother's neighbors and more difficult for her caregivers. His children, and others in my own family, thought the solution should be a nursing home for both of them, saying "She would want the relationship, no matter what." But I knew her first priority had always been staying in the residence. It was decided that the boyfriend would have to move out.

Others brought up how her caregiving was expensive and was likely to deprive her children of elements of inheritance. Again, some urged she be moved to an assisted living facility. "Wouldn't she be happier with all that nice company?" Still, her priorities guided the decision, and she was pleased to stay in the apartment as planned. (It's also worth emphasizing that maximizing wealth for her children was never mentioned as one of her priorities.)

Her priorities, clearly and often articulated and discussed, gave my family the information we needed to make choices for her. We rested easily knowing those choices were what she truly wanted. By openly and honestly discussing my mother's priorities with her, I was able to push and pull at what she was saying, resulting in a true conversation. That back-and-forth ensured she understood the implications and possible eventualities of her choices. And as mentioned, we were also able to revisit and monitor those priorities from time to time. Of course, my mother is not the only wise woman who has had such forethought. There are many others who have insisted on staying in their home as their top priority.

Another wise woman, my grandmother, decided—at age seventy—that she would stay in her own house in her golden years. The home was large, with an elevator and many floors, and the house itself was in a neighborhood that had once been grand but had fallen on hard times. Still, she had no interest in moving. She was an artist, and she loved to go into her basement studio late at night to paint alone in her empty house.

"I live for my painting, and I paint in solitude," she told her children "My priority is to stay in this house until I die, and I want you to support me in this plan."

"But what if you fall and it takes days for someone to find you?" asked her daughter.

"I am willing to risk that to maintain my independence," was her mother's reply.

My grandmother's wise children balanced the support they wanted to provide their mother against the danger solitude might present. They also considered their mother's decision that she was willing to take the risk inherent in living alone at that age. She willingly sacrificed her personal safety to retain the independence she wanted to continue painting. Rather than trying to control her life's wishes, my father and his siblings opted to support my grandmother in her wishes, and my grandmother lived in her house into her late eighties. She never fell, and she died in her sleep—a happy ending to her life's story.

In contrast with these wise women, an elderly gentleman who came to my office in St. Louis was perfectly happy not to have *anyone* help him with his priorities and planning. He believed political chaos in the US was inevitable, and he feared a Communist takeover of the world. To prepare, his top priority was to store away adequate financial resources. He had arranged a safe deposit box in a Swiss bank and placed $10 million of gold bullion in it. He would access that wealth if and, according to him, when the time came. No one was to know about that box except himself.

"What about your son?" I asked. His son was helping him run his business and affairs, and I assumed he was a likely confidante.

"Oh no," said the old man. "The Communists will end up getting information out of him by threatening his family. I can't tell him about that gold."

His strategy of secrecy seemed to make sense to him until I asked, "Suppose you are too old to travel? Suppose you suffer dementia or memory loss? What if you die?"

There was silence. Then he said, "Let me think about that." The next day he called to tell me he had shared all of this information with his son, who had promised not to let "them" torture it out of him. Only then could an actual strategy be developed, and a plan implemented that would allow the wealth to survive in the event of the old man's incapacity.

UPDATING PRIORITIES

Priorities can change with age and circumstance, so there is no reason to cast them in stone. In fact, they always need regular review, as I did with my mother. Along those lines, an elderly client—an artist with a coterie of good friends and students—had always told me as her trustee that her highest priorities were creating art as long as possible and maintaining her relationships with her students and friends. She loved teaching just as much as she loved having company as she worked. She had even designed her apartment with a studio in a way that allowed others to participate in her artistic process. To accomplish her priorities, she planned to stay in that apartment indefinitely. "I want to live fully and for many years with my art and friends, and that is my highest priority," she often said.

I visited her one day when she was in her late eighties. She had just returned from a week's stay in the hospital, where she had been recovering from pneumonia. She looked me in the eye and said, "My priorities have changed. I have a new highest priority: never ever to spend another night in a hospital."

I listened quietly, before saying, "But if you need to be in a hospital you will have to go, yes?"

She replied, "No, I will not."

Three weeks later she was found in her studio, slumped over, and the life gone from her, an apparent heart attack. She never spent another night in the hospital. That artist was clear on her priority. I was clear on it as well, but I had no idea how to help her meet her goal if she needed hospitalization.

Another client was active, engaged, and had a zest and passion for life. In her youth, she often exclaimed, "I never want to be too old to enjoy life." Her friends and I understood that her highest priority was living life to the fullest. In fact, she had a priority similar to that of the artist, but that priority emerged only as she got older. At age sixty, and almost out of the blue, she said to me, "I never want to see a doctor again."

The older she was, the more she repeated that sentiment. I concluded that this was one priority I could not help her accomplish. She was relatively young and quite independent, so I assumed she was managing her own affairs and living her life, even if avoiding doctors. Indeed, I thought to myself that her statements were the almost playful attitude of an aging eccentric.

I lost touch with her for five weeks. I went to her house, called her phone, and found her nowhere. Shortly after I had given up on the search, I got a call from a neighbor of mine. It turned out my client had been cared for in his house and had died that morning.

"Of what?" I asked.

"Oh, we don't know," said the neighbor. "She never wanted you to know that she was a Christian Scientist, as are we. We do not consult medical doctors at all." That woman needed my neighbor to help her accomplish her goal. He could help her; I could not.

Priorities can also change if you find you cannot execute those you had set. For example, a friend was a very successful competitive long-distance runner. Her No. 1 priority was running and competing well into her old age. She had planned everything around that priority: Where she lived, how she ate, and even where she went for vacations to ensure she had access to running tracks or paths while there. One day she called me to say her doctor said she could no longer perform any strenuous exercise.

"He tells me my heart will not take it, and frankly, my knees are bothering me as well." I told her I was sorry, and she said, "But with what I know and how I have lived, I want to take up coaching young people." Coaching young athletes became her priority, and she redesigned her old age around helping others learn how to be marathon runners.. That friend was wise. Her story illustrates the necessity of reevaluating priorities and maintaining the flexibility to transition from one to another. After all, she might have simply announced that if she could no longer run, she might as well finish life sitting on a couch reflecting on the fun she had as a runner.

Help in Setting and Maintaining Priorities

Priorities are best developed through a deliberate, careful, and often guided process. When developing these priorities and strategies, a *support team* needs to be engaged. They can help you articulate the priorities and consider the various possible impediments you might encounter. That team may consist of some or all of your family members. Or it may include lawyers, doctors, geriatric social workers, clergy or spiritual leaders, or friends. (We will explore some of those professionals and how to work with them in Chapter 3.) It may be all of the above, but the process is important.

This team will become your *helping hands*, the support group that will enable you to continue your chase. The ancient Roman Appius had a household to do so; Shakespeare's King Lear had his beloved daughter, Cordelia. These types of caring confidantes are crucial to maintaining your standard of living, but these helping hands also need preparation to assist you. As discussed, you will therefore need to communicate your intent and plan, so your priorities can be understood and seamlessly carried out.

Most importantly, helping hands must always understand that their role is one of *support*, not control. Unfortunately, the two may get muddled. Often, a support team believes they are doing the right thing by making decisions for the people they are supposed to be supporting, instead of honoring decisions and goals. Typically, your support team wants to be helpful, but they often end up viewing their role as protecting you from harm and ensuring your safety. But helping hands need to understand the difference between genuine support and burdensome control.

Members of the support team need to have had the conversations and reached a clear understanding about how the aging person would want safety to be considered. The helping hands are not to be asked whether they endorse the priorities of the person they support or how they might decide to change them. Rather, they need to *understand* the priorities and confirm that the strategies can ultimately be implemented, even when the aging person cannot implement them. Again, this role is one of support, *not* control.

A wonderful example of a helping hand is a story about one of my father's clients. The man was one of the wealthiest men in his community but was little known. His helping hand was his son, who had inherited some wealth, but nothing as substantial as the wealth he would ultimately inherit after his father died. The old man collected certain artifacts and regularly went to a dealer specializing in them. One day my father saw the old man leaving the dealer's shop. When my father went in, the dealer took him aside and said, "You probably don't know that old man, though you may have heard of his wealthy son." Before my father had the chance to reply, the dealer continued:. "And what a wonderful son he is! He has great wealth, and the old man appears not to."

"Actually," my father began to say, but then he paused, curious to hear what the dealer was about to tell him.

"The old man regularly comes in to buy artifacts," said the dealer, "And when I set a price for one, he always counters with a ridiculously low price, telling me he could not afford the price I've set. But his son privately told me to accept whatever the old man wants, and I do."

"Why's that?" my father asked

"Well, the son then comes by every week and always pays

me the difference. How fortunate the old man is in the son's love—and wealth."

The old man never knew that his son was actually facilitating his collection. Instead of telling his father what to spend or how, this good son gave the man free reign to strike a deal and enjoy himself in the process. Rather than being outwardly controlling, the son was clever. He enabled his father's passion, which allowed the old man to continue his mission and fuel his optimism. In fact, the son was probably overpaying the dealer, but it was not financially harmful. As long as the father didn't know it, it would not hurt his self-esteem. Ultimately, as in this case, your support team needs to understand your dream and how it can be actualized, even into old age. This support is absolutely necessary to pursue your life's passions.

Conclusion

Ensuring you can do what you want in your old age does not happen by itself. You must start by deciding on your priorities. You need to define and understand these priorities, analyze what might keep you from pursuing them, and consider ways to avoid any obstacles. Such consideration requires helping hands as you develop and decide how to implement strategies. Priorities and strategies need to be reviewed as your life circumstances change since those changes may make implementation impossible, or may change the way you think about what is important to you. With deliberation and the help of your support team, you are likely to set the dreams you want to chase and have the helping hands necessary to support you in that chase well into old age.

CHAPTER 2
EXECUTIVE FUNCTION: LIVING WELL AS YOUR BRAIN AGES

Some of us grow old with a superb memory intact. There are those of us who, even as we age, maintain an uncanny ability to know where we have placed a shred of paper on a desk full of confusion, or that one wooden spoon in a kitchen with no apparent order. These people amaze their spouses and friends and are the envy of those accustomed to slips in their own memory—forgetting where they put an important document among clutter, the salt on the spice rack, or their favorite pair of shoes. Yet even those with that uncanny ability to remember where everything is often end up requiring help as they get older. One husband and wife were fortunate in this way for many years. Though he kept everything carefully ordered to help him find whatever he needed, she, without any apparent organization, could find everything just as easily. But as she aged, some of that sharp memory dulled.

As she entered her seventies, her abilities dwindled, and without ever worrying much about organization before, she had a hard time adjusting. She could find seemingly nothing. Though her husband's memory weakened as well, he was not at the same disadvantage. He knew that every object had its place, every paper fit into a clear order. He also took notes and placed them where he could find them, then disposed of them when finished. His wife tried following his lead—scattering notes and lists about the house—but failed entirely. Her memory got worse, and though they would have successfully organized and moved out of their house in their sixties, they no longer could. Waiting until she was in her seventies made it almost impossible to organize and pack all their belongings. In the end, they moved into an assisted-living facility, but only with the help of concerned family members.

Often, with old age, it is our family who first notices our declining mental capacities. It is not uncommon to hear them say things like, "What do we do about father? He has started to lose his ability to understand his own affairs but won't recognize that." Or "Mother repeats herself over and over again. It drives me nuts, but she doesn't seem to remember what she's said. What should we do?" A doctor friend of mine says that whenever children come to his office to note items a parent is forgetting, he knows that memory problems are certain: "The kids are never wrong."

Unfortunately, we cannot stop the progression of aging. That much is clear, but it should also be clear that we can prepare ourselves for aging to continue to take full advantage of our lives. Perhaps nowhere is preparation more necessary, and less frequently addressed, than the loss of executive function—the ability to make rational and competent decisions for yourself or others as you age.

Though executive function has overtones of business acumen and the ability to engage in commerce of one kind or another, the loss of this capability (whether forgetfulness, dementia, or senility) diminishes your ability to live a full life—to chase your dream in old age. Diminished executive function or capacity can happen almost imperceptibly over time. For colleagues, family members, and others close to the person it affects, the condition always seems to get more and more difficult. The aging person may be aware of it—or not. Yet, no matter how it happens, it always presents new problems and challenges, both for the person affected, and the people around them.

We all hear the stories about 100-year-olds who are as alert and capable as they were in their twenties. In reality, statistics indicate those people are few and far between. Indeed, according to the Alzheimer's association, one in three senior Americans will die of Alzheimer's or another form of dementia.[2] Inevitably, there is likely to be some loss of "function" as you age. Whether it reaches dementia or simply stays as forgetfulness or loss of judgment, there is a good chance it will happen. Although the loss of capacity typically takes place gradually, it is also possible for a person to be 100 percent capable one day and completely incompetent the next.

Alas, aging carries with it the distressing thought that loss of executive capacity is a real possibility. As with many aspects of your ability to continue your chase, preparation for this eventuality is critical. Regardless of when and how you might lose executive function, you must start planning while you're still sharp and capable. Before developing the plan, you need to first understand the critical related issues and how they may affect you.

DEMENTIA AND ALZHEIMER'S

Dementia brings loss of executive function by limiting an individual's faculties, capabilities, and engagement in everyday activities. Speaking from my own experience with clients facing dementia, the condition may take many forms, and has many underlying causes. I have clients who can reason carefully. However, once they lose that chain of reasoning, they cannot remember where and how they got to their decisions. Others cycle their ideas and statements over and over. Many ask the same questions, coming to the same answer every time. Some clients recall details from years earlier, but they cannot remember what happened the day before. Others refer to "senior moments" and complain they cannot think of names of their business associates, acquaintances, and even friends and family. What all of these clients have in common is that they, or their families, feel varying degrees of insecurity. That often leads to worry about how reasonably and safely they can make good decisions or engage in life.

I often see clients consult physicians on account of memory "issues." Many leave their appointments with a clean bill of health. Unfortunately, many others do not. Ten years before her death, a client's son called to tell me that his mother was having "memory issues" and he and his sister had taken her to a specialist for examination. The doctor ran tests and concluded she was on a steady decline, likely Alzheimer's, he surmised. Going forward, he examined her once a year, and though she didn't decline much further, she had limited competence for the next ten years until her death.

That client had no understanding of her own condition. After her first session with the doctor, she reported to me that she had a "tiny bit of a memory problem but nothing to worry about." Even as she received written reports from the doctor about her condition and the likelihood that it was Alzheimer's disease, she repeated (often over and over) that she had no such issue and was perfectly capable. She lived happily those ten years, completely oblivious to her mental limitations, always cheerful and surrounded by friends and family.

Another client was diagnosed as "pre-Alzheimer's" and gradually lost all short-term memory. For many years, his competency was not markedly different from that of the woman with a "tiny bit" of a problem, yet, he was acutely and painfully aware he had dementia and recognized his reasoning and memory were unreliable. He was unhappy. Any time he had visitors, he would explain he had memory issues and he should not be relied on. Ultimately, he spent all of his time at home staring into space, lamenting his condition.

So, is it better to be happily oblivious like the woman I described, or is it better to know you are developing dementia like the man, spending your days brooding? For the aging wealth holder, I believe the former is preferable. For your family members, advisors, or caregivers, it is unclear. The former requires much more patience by family members and caregivers trying to support the patient. The latter requires that the aged person receive psychological counseling and possibly treatment for depression. I have both kinds of clients. Frankly, I find it easier to work with those oblivious to their condition than those stuck in dark unhappiness because of it.

If you could be certain you would maintain full faculties and awareness and never suffer dementia before the moment of death, much of your planning would not be necessary. But you have to be realistic. That's why most of the strategy and planning for aging contemplates that a person may start to lose capacity, either because of physical disability or mental incompetence. That planning requires careful consideration of the risks involved.

RISKS

There are five primary risks regarding the loss of executive function. These risks are the same whether you have full blown dementia (or not) and whether you are aware of your decline (or not):

1. Emotional paralysis can result from fear and insecurity over your condition. (But if you are oblivious to the condition, you will avoid this risk.)
2. Your behavior can create physical danger for yourself or others.
3. Financial matters can be mishandled, resulting in the loss of money for you and any of your potential heirs.
4. Your relationships with others—family, business associates, friends—can become confused and badly impacted.
5. Your reputation in the community can be irredeemably harmed.

Each of these risks should be evaluated separately and then collectively in contemplating strategies and you should realize that the risks are not mutually exclusive. Though these risks are all discussed in the following chapters, one that often comes up regularly for wealthy individuals and their families is the financial fallout resulting from financial mismanagement. Financial mismanagement can indeed be devastating for the elderly wealth holder and the family.

An older woman I knew—always capable and quite computer literate—received a call one morning from her "computer virus protection program." The caller claimed her software license had expired and needed renewal. She gave her credit card number over the phone and was told to wait a few days for "restoration" of the protection. Two days later, she received a second call from a "desperate" customer agent who told her he had lost her card number and was about to be fired. The only solution, he said, was for her to send $30,000 to him in cash. That way, he could salvage his position in the company.

Outrageous as that should have sounded, she sent him $30,000 in cash via Federal Express overnight delivery. Three days later, she called me to say she needed another $50,000 in cash. They had contacted her once again. She asked me to tell her bank to move the funds to her checking account. Asking her to explain her situation, I learned of the entire fraud. Of course, I did not give her the $50,000 in cash and instead sent fraud experts to look into the matter. She was out $30,000 but not $80,000.

Hard as it may be to believe, she called my firm again the next week. She said PayPal had mixed up her account and wanted her to send $50,000 in cash to repay an erroneous credit to her account. This was, of course, another fraud, but one that we avoided. We were able to design protections and backstops to help her avoid these scams. Today, she has all sorts of safeguards built into her relationship with her bank and custodian. For her safety, her bank accounts are now completely protected by a requirement that her co-trustee, a professional, approve every expenditure. Over the past year, hardly a week goes by without her calling to say she needs cash immediately for some fraudulent scheme being perpetrated on her. She has no recollection of the scheme the prior week (or her initial loss of $30,000).

The elderly are quite susceptible to fraud. As we age, we can lose the ability to spot unreasonable and criminal intent, and sending $30,000 in cash from a phone request somehow ends up seeming reasonable. Luckily, protections can be built into our affairs to limit financial damage. These safeguards include maximum credit card charge limits, checks requiring two signatures, and limited access to credit cards, social security cards, and similar identification items.

Three of the other risks—physical, relationships, and reputational—can also be managed with sound process. For reputation, for instance, the use of durable powers of attorney can help. Careful selection of one's trustees and attorneys can be part of the solution. Ensuring succession in business can also be essential. Setting up careful mailing and communication with various boards can further protect your reputation. Perhaps the most challenging risk, though, is managing the depression and fear that can grip you when you are aware of your condition. That management generally requires caring support and often psychiatric attention and medication. Preparing for that condition is difficult, and not terribly productive, but must be considered.

No matter how the risks are handled, *they must be addressed*, however distressing this task may be. When you have lost executive function, it will be too late to discuss the risks reasonably and comfortably. I'm reminded of a son who said to his father, "Hey dad, I'm sorry but you have lost your executive function. You can no longer deal with your colleagues and friends without assistance." You can imagine how effective that was. It was a pointless statement that ruined a relationship and could have been avoided with some proper planning. Indeed, when planning for your own diminished metal capabilities, you will need help and care, just as you will when setting your priorities and having them honored (as discussed in Chapter 1).

Planning Ahead

Loss of executive function and the related issues have been extensively studied and written about. Surprisingly, it is still not easy to find guidance to manage this problem for yourself or your aging loved ones. Yes, family doctors relay stories of patients who worry about their memories; geriatric medicine is expanding its capability to deal with dementia; and geriatric social workers are more popular today than ever before (more on geriatric social workers in Chapter 3). However, few young people—presumably many years from loss of executive function—carefully plan strategies to deal with its decay or loss.

Preparation for that loss is crucial and should include looking at various protective strategies. Further, those who love or advise you will need advance planning and those strategies as much as you do. If you and they end up needing these strategies, you will be glad you developed them. If you never need the strategies, you are fortunate indeed! With that in mind, let us start by outlining a number of the easy steps.

While still fully capable, finish the following legal documents, which can help protect you against one or more of the previously mentioned risks.

- Durable powers of attorneys to name people to act for you in business and financial matters if you cannot.
- Durable powers of attorney for healthcare to allow someone to make your healthcare decisions when you cannot. (These people may be different from those who will act on your behalf regarding financial matters.)

- The authority to allow your chosen representatives to talk to your doctors (so-called "HIPAA Waivers").
- Living wills and similar documents to express your wishes relating to final health support.
- Letters of wishes to memorialize your desires (though these are seen as optional by most people).
- Revocable trusts to hold your investment and business assets.

All of these documents, except the last two, are fairly standard. Indeed, hospitals and doctors frequently provide them. Letters of wishes can be written at home at your convenience and without any legal language. In fact, the document that deserves the most attention is the revocable trust.

REVOCABLE TRUSTS

Revocable Trusts are usually recommended by lawyers as a way to avoid probate at your death. With a well-designed revocable trust augmented by joint ownership and accounts payable at death—along with similar forms of ownership—your heirs (and your attorneys) will never have the inconvenience of dealing with probate courts. As the term is used here, a revocable trust is one you (as "grantor" or "settlor") create during your lifetime and into which you place most, if not all, of your property. During your lifetime, you retain the right to modify or revoke the trust at any time prior to your death. You can change your mind as often as you like, so that your direction of gifts and bequests works just like a will. Note, it is *critical* to title the assets in the exact name of the trust. Otherwise, the assets will be subject to probate, which can involve significant expense and delays. Any attorney can ensure the assets are properly titled.

Avoiding probate may make life easier for your lawyers and cheaper for your heirs, but since you won't be there, this streamlined process will make little difference to you. The most valuable benefit for you is that a revocable trust will establish a management succession of your affairs during your lifetime. Since loss of function is typically gradual, the continuity of your financial affairs is essential. A revocable trust allows for the management of your assets and the provision of support over that time.

With a revocable trust, you will want to select trustees in addition to, or aside from, yourself. This person or people—your co-trustee or co-trustees—will effectively act as your successor if you lose the ability to manage the trust and your financial affairs. Naming yourself as the only trustee until you are incapacitated is not the best way to ensure seamless succession. If you are the only trustee, incapacity will require that you or someone else (the successor trustee) remove and replace you. Such action may require a doctor's certificate or even a court proceeding. Removal will be painful if you understand what is happening and difficult emotionally—and practically—for the person removing you. Further, if your decline is gradual, someone will have to determine a precise moment when you become incapable of handling your own affairs.

Therefore, instead of serving as your own sole trustee, you should consider a co-trustee to serve with you, *starting when you create the trust*. Because you have the power to amend the trust, you can always change the person you have selected as co-trustee. However, as you begin losing executive function, your co-trustee can continue to act with you, remaining a trustee for some period and gradually assuming more of the duties with or without your engagement. (This approach has proven extremely helpful for many of my clients.) The revocable trust can stipulate that any action taken by the trust creator will govern as if the creator were sole trustee. But if you find yourself sending $30,000 in cash by FedEx to an anonymous caller, the trust can be modified to provide that no action will be valid without the consent of the co-trustee. So not only does the revocable trust end up avoiding probate, it also protects you against your gradual incapacity. Deciding on the co-trustee, however, takes careful consideration.

CHOOSING TRUSTEES AND CO-TRUSTEES

A husband and wife had two children, a son in the family business and a daughter who was an artist. The daughter, a spendthrift, became angry with her father whenever he did not meet her supposed financial "needs." Meanwhile, the son was a responsible support for both parents. When the father died, he left his estate in a trust for his widow and children. He named his son as a co-trustee with his widow, knowing that with two trustees, both would have to agree to any distribution from the trust.

The daughter, then in her fifties, resented the arrangement and told her mother so. She wanted to be a trustee, and she thought it only fair if she could take money from the trust whenever she wanted. Though she had no choice but to accept her father's wishes, she repeatedly told her mother the decision was "unfair" and regularly asked for more money from the trust. After each demand, the mother said to her son, "I don't want to give her money. Next thing I know, she'll be emptying the trust and leaving me nothing. That's why your father set up the trust as he did in the first place. He wanted to make sure I had the funds to live my life. But I also don't want to refuse your sister. Whenever I do, she responds with such angry threats. The whole situation makes me very unhappy."

Luckily, as the co-trustee, the son took on communication with his sister regarding the trust. After all, without his consent to any gift or payment, she could not receive any money from the trust. In a way, the mother put her son in his father's position as the person who said no. Living up to his responsibility, he handled the exchanges with his sister whenever his mother wanted to resist an entreaty. The mother could then commiserate with her daughter, and together they could blame the son for frustrating his sister's desires. The son didn't mind, and he was happy to help.

Of course, this is not the only example of such an arrangement. It is not unusual to require the approval of a co-trustee when another trustee (or the creator of the revocable trust) becomes vulnerable to pressures from within, or outside, the family. As my firm has seen over many decades, family dynamics can get messy. To avoid potentially sticky situations among relatives, it's often best to put a trustee or co-trustee in place that is not a family member. Instead, leave that task to a trusted advisor or assistant.

A businessman of immense wisdom, respected throughout his community, sold his family business when he was forty years old. He had created great wealth for the whole family—his wife, his five children, his brother and sister-in-law, and himself. He strategically planned how to handle this new wealth, administering all of the family's funds. The man also carefully designed investment plans and selected top-tier managers. The result: the family prospered, and their wealth grew. Unfortunately, they were visited by problems, including addiction and mental health issues. Meanwhile, none of the children worked, and as the patriarch, the father bore the full burden of caring for everyone. It was hard, but he still managed to engage fully in his community. He served on boards, assumed leadership roles, and was generally a model citizen, giving back through his wisdom and philanthropy.

About his finances, the wealth holder detested banks and was therefore determined one would never take charge of his portfolio. Indeed, his mantra for the family wealth was, "No bank will ever have anything to do with our family money." His loyal assistant—who had started in the business when she was finishing high school and stayed on as his "secretary"—understood his priority, and she worked with a team of advisors he had hired to achieve that outcome. His wife was not involved in the financial management, and his five children paid no attention, even though he repeatedly recited that mantra for the family wealth: No Bank.

As mentioned, he was a strategic thinker and a wise man; that was, until it came to selecting his co-trustees. Although none of his children was in the family business, he felt that, because he loved them, they should be his co-trustees—all together. The suggestion that he might consider naming his loyal assistant as a trustee was met with reluctance. "She will be there to help them," he said, "but they are my children—she is not."

As he aged, his memory started fading and his mental capabilities became weaker and weaker. One of his children got divorced and lost much of his money in the process. Unable or unwilling to find a full-time job, that child asked for money from his father. The father obliged. So the son continued asking for money, over and over. "He needs it," was the father's reasoning, "And I have plenty." Realizing the trust was finite and that the son seemed to be blowing through it, the assistant did what she could to slow the "gifts" down.

However, there seemed to be no question that the father wanted to continue supporting his son. According to his other children, that was not enough. Led by his eldest daughter, his children said that it was important that there be "equality" of distribution among the children and the struggling son should "go get a job." The children began fighting with each other, some demanding that the favored son return any money received. It did not matter to them that the father had good reason in his own mind to help his unfortunate child.

The father, caught up in the middle of the squabbling, was unable to understand what was happening or figure out how to restore order among his family. His executive function was diminishing. As the fighting continued, four of the children went to court in their roles as trustees to stop the outflow to the fifth. Litigation followed. The court restored order by removing the father and his children as trustees and replacing them with the very entity the father dreaded most—a bank. The bank reoriented the portfolio, and the bankers concluded that the employment of the man's long-time, trusted assistant was too extravagant and unnecessary. They even moved the man and his wife into a nursing home ("much more efficient," according to the trust officer and four of the children). The unfortunate son and the loyal assistant objected, but no one listened.

The man's mistake was in selecting all of his children as the co-trustees of his revocable trust without realizing they were not professionally or emotionally equipped to manage that role. In truth, his assistant would have been the right choice to ensure that his financial affairs were handled as he would have wanted. As he grew older and less capable, she had worked with him gently and carefully to help him retire from a number of boards before his weaknesses were too visible. She could have managed the financial affairs just as deftly as she wound down his board service. She knew him and how to protect him.

This story demonstrates that the selection of your co-trustee, or the succession of trustees, is as important as anything you can do in planning for advancing age. It is central to designing a good governance. Whether a family member or trusted assistant, choose wisely early on, unclouded by sentimentality. Replacing that trustee will be a real challenge when you are not capable. If you choose multiple co-trustees, consider the role each will play, such as the son's support of his mother when his sister harassed her for money. And recognize that though you may *want* to appoint family members as trustees, they are not always the best choice. By securing the trust under someone who best understands such matters—and knows your personal thoughts when you are of sound mind—you will help all of the trust beneficiaries.

Determining the best trustee is a frequent challenge, as my firm has seen many times over the years. One husband and wife spent years trying to decide who should be trustees after they were both deceased. They had two children—a son and a daughter—and could not agree whether both of them, one of them, or neither of them made sense as trustees. After years of indecision, they created and funded a lifetime trust irrevocably. It was ostensibly intended for tax planning purposes, but as the husband noted, it was also "for a test run." They named the two children to serve with a professional trustee. While the husband and wife were still alive, they wanted to see how the children would perform. In fact, the children were not good trustees. They couldn't reach decisions, and they felt uncomfortable in their roles as trustees. Trustee meetings lasted for hours, and investment managers could not be selected. The process was tense. The children, who had once gotten along well, started arguing and had no empathy for each other.

Ultimately that "test run trust" was forcibly ended. The parents concluded quite wisely that neither child should be a trustee and that their own trusts should have professional trustees after their deaths. The "test run trust" had miserable investment performance—stuck in treasury bonds as the equity markets soared. Yet, the husband has said the trust was "the best trust" he had ever created because it helped him figure out who should be his trustees.

MUTUAL SUPPORT

The people who plan to support you will need advance planning just as much as you will if you lose your executive function. Consider the ninety-year-old dentist in Chapter 1 who said he would let me know if he were to quit practicing dentistry. He and his son should have discussed his legacy and how to preserve it as he aged. How much better it would have been for the dentist's son to know he was fulfilling his father's wishes as he closed the business.

In dealing with those losing capability, a key distinction, raised in Chapter 1, lies in the difference between control and support. An aging parent losing capacity wants to be supported, not *controlled* by a child, just as a child wants to be supported, not controlled, by a parent. An advisor who tries to "control" his client will likely be fired before the advisor accomplishes much. That said, the difference between "control" and "support" is often more about perception than reality when it comes to executive function.

An example of a supportive approach involved a large

revocable trust with two trustees, the grantor (the wealthy individual) and his advisor. The trust said that the grantor could act as the sole trustee. He therefore had complete legal control of the trust. In the early years, when the grantor was in his fifties, he made all decisions relating to investments and similar matters. His advisor was nowhere to be seen. As the grantor entered his seventies, he began to be susceptible to salesmen of less than the highest integrity. As deals "too good to be passed up" were presented, he proudly introduced the salesmen to his advisor.

The advisor never called out the salesmen. Instead, he treated the grantor with great respect and prepared an analysis to serve as a basis for discussing how the investment would fit into their asset allocation. The advisor told the grantor, "This investment really looks good, but it does not meet your needs in terms of asset allocation, risk tolerance, and other related factors. Of course, the decision is still up to you." He left the grantor feeling in control—the grantor would decide for himself if the salesmen could be dismissed on the basis that the investment was not appropriate for the grantor's overall plan.

As the grantor became less and less capable, the advisor increased the frequency of their visits, explaining to the grantor that his wisdom should be shared with his advisor "just in case" the grantor became incapacitated. Before long, everything was a "joint" consideration to ensure that the grantor's thinking, and way of working, could be imparted to his advisor for future generations. The advisor repeatedly used the word "support" when he met with the grantor. Eventually, as the grantor became less capable, he also became less interested in handling the family finances. The advisor made more and more decisions, each of which was initially shared with the grantor as an "idea" for consideration. The advisor left the grantor always feeling in control, with the advisor in the secondary role of mentee and student.

The children of aging wealth holders are not always as wise. How often I have heard clients say, "Who does my daughter think she is? This is my life, and she is trying to control me." I never hear, "My daughter is offering to support me or help me, and I resent that." How much more effective that daughter would be if she were seen as offering "support" to her father, particularly as he begins to feel the uncertainties of old age.

Support can come in many ways. It can be a simple trip to the grocery by a son or a friend, or the arrangement for delivery of a special meal. Support can even be planned for in advance as a joint effort between the aging person and his "helping hand." I hear this frequently: "Often when we are at a party, my husband says something and then repeats himself shortly after. He doesn't realize he is repeating himself. If I try to tell him in front of others, he is embarrassed." Similarly, there are the spouses who unknowingly start talking almost incessantly, also embarrassing themselves. For years, I thought there was no easy solution to this common problem, until I spoke to a geriatric social worker about the subject.

She explained that in early stages of mental decline, people who repeat themselves may not realize they are doing so, and they do not welcome the "public" rebuke from a spouse or family member. She recommended developing a code word. This word is a relatively insignificant one that can be easily recognized, letting someone know if he or she is repeating the same story or words or is acting otherwise unreasonably. Used once in the conversation, the word will encourage the speaker to be more careful about repetition, interrupting others, or causing any other kind of embarrassment. The code word is especially helpful in early stages of loss of executive function. By developing one with your helping hands, they can provide you with a simple, supportive reminder when necessary.

Ultimately, what you want, and what your family and advisors want, is for you to continue living the life you envisioned in old age, one that is full of joy and contentment, no matter your executive function. Just as you have likely supported your loved ones throughout their lives, they—or the people of your choosing—should be there to support you in your most difficult times as you age.

CONCLUSION

One of the challenges to aging is the loss of executive function, which usually sneaks up on you and can derail all of your plans and aspirations. It can't be reasoned with, and so far, it is almost impossible to cure. It is likely to strike when you are eager to focus on what you want to do most in life, and it will distract you from that focus, if not prevent it altogether. But you and your family and advisors can plan to minimize its effect by developing strategies before you start to suffer. Together, you can minimize its interference. No matter who you are, you need to start planning for the potential loss of mental function. If you're lucky enough to maintain all your faculties, then you are lucky indeed, but if you do lose some or all of your cognitive ability, planning will have been well worth your time. And your family, advisors, and caregivers will be grateful.

CHAPTER 3
EXPERTS: ENHANCING YOUR SUPPORT TEAM

A single woman I knew in her late seventies devoted herself to helping a small school for children with disabilities. Though she appeared to have little money, she was, in fact, quite wealthy. She could have spent her time travelling, dining at high-end restaurants, doing anything wealth allows, but she was inspired by, and devoted to, this school. Her volunteer work there started one day when her church sewing group toured the school. It seemed like a great place for the students, but it was also somewhat shabby and in disrepair. After the tour, she went to the principal and said, "Your curtains are really quite ragged. Would you mind if I worked on new ones?" He readily agreed, and she spent a year sewing and hanging curtains at the school. The next year, she began another sewing project, volunteering at the school three days a week. By the time she was in her mid-eighties, she regularly helped clean up the school's class-rooms, grounds, and hallways. It wasn't what would normally be considered appropriate work for a woman her age and with her wealth, but she loved it. And the school was completely unaware that she had any wealth at all but valued her volunteerism and devotion to the school and its students.

One day, I asked her why she was performing such hard work when she could have simply donated money to the school instead (she had an ample amount). "You would have me wake up every morning and write a check, sitting on the sidelines simply donating money and waiting to die?" she asked. "If I were to do that, I wouldn't get the chance to watch those children succeed with my help. By devoting my days to that school, I make a real impact on those kids' lives. Nothing has ever brought me such joy. I will give the school money when the time comes." When she died at ninety, she left her $5 million fortune to the school surprising the school entirely and increasing its endowment considerably.

That woman had a mission that gave her the optimism to carry on a fulfilling life. Her tasks were not complex, and she was able to perform them until she died. At her own home, she had a full-time housekeeper and would never wash a sink or vacuum the floor there. Her real passion was providing a clean environment for those children, not cleaning her own home, so she focused on that goal. A wise woman, she hired financial advisors and managers to handle her fortune. That ensured the school would end up with substantial wealth once she was gone. By having clear priorities and delegating tasks to trusted experts, she supported the school both during *and* after her life.

Experts—whether housekeepers or wealth managers—can create the flexibility you may need to chase your dream. Aging with freedom, therefore, requires differentiating between the truly important and the not-so-important—between what you want to do, or can do, and what you do not want to do, or cannot do. Activities you don't want to, or are unable to, handle can be taken care of by others. Why should tasks you don't enjoy occupy your increasingly limited time on Earth? It's critical to find those people to whom you can comfortably and confidently delegate the minutiae and complexities of life that are not of interest to you or may require professionals.

Unwanted tasks can be taken off your plate with a little forethought. If you love cooking, for example, you may like preparing extravagant dinners for friends and family but abhor the clean-up afterward. A friend of mine found himself in this exact position. As a man of means, however, he hired a helper to come to his house as he cooked and serve as his "sous chef"— mainly a dishwasher. Your wealth can often easily help you build the resources you need, whether a "sous chef," a pilot for a private plane, or an expert money manager.

The challenge, of course, is that delegating tasks isn't always easy. Wealth holders, and frankly, most people, consider themselves experts on most subjects. My children would call us "control freaks." In our thirties and forties, we feel like we are in control of our lives. We are always present, always in charge. With age though, even intense control freaks can slowly lose control of more and more aspects of their lives. Earlier rather than later, we need to assemble the support team of trusted advisors, discussed in Chapter 1, to whom we can also pass tasks or projects that are not high priorities. Aging well requires an early recognition that you will need support from that team. But you may need more. You (and that support team) often need to hire expert help as well.

HIRING EXPERTS

It's essential to build your core group of advisors and helping hands over time. It's also wise to let them know your priorities early on and then gradually delegate tasks you can no longer, or no longer want to, manage yourself. Choosing that team will take a lot of thought, and no team is likely to have all the necessary expertise for every daily activity. After you have assembled your team, together, you should identify the necessary resources and most effective way to access them. These resources may include anything from medical professionals to lawyers to catering services to housecleaners. You may also need to engage companies that can find the right help. Indeed, sometimes the experts need to hire experts themselves.

WHEN TO HIRE EXPERTS

When should you or your team consider an expert, and where should you turn? Here are a few rules of thumb to consider. A common refrain among lawyers is that the lawyer who represents himself has a fool for a client. The psychiatrist attempting to treat his own family's dysfunction will likely fail. And so it goes. One of my clients was a world-renowned surgeon who had spent his career diagnosing heart disease and performing heart surgery. When he recognized symptoms of heart disease in himself, he guided his treatment until he ultimately needed surgery. At that point, he wisely engaged another surgeon to perform the operation. This was one task he could not do on his own.

A client of mine in his late sixties with a Ph.D. in economics wanted a house that would perfectly fulfill his needs. "I want my home soon, so I can spend my final years in it. I know exactly what I want," he said. After finding a plot of land to build the house, he needed an architect and contractor to get the project started. However, he decided to act as his own "project manager" and oversee much of the construction himself. At the outset, the economist boasted to me: "I'm a bright man—I can figure this out. What can a tradesperson do that I couldn't? I'm sure managing this project will be simple."

Three years later, the house was unbuilt. Not surprisingly, the project had run into some major problems, and the economist had no idea what he was doing. The contractor told the economist that certain details of the architect's plans were simply unrealistic. The contractor also said the costs were running well beyond estimates. At the rate the project was going, it would take at least five years to complete. That's when the Ph.D. had his brightest idea: He needed an expert. He found a construction manager who, though he did not have a Ph.D. in economics, pulled everything together and got the project back on track. Of course, this was at considerable expense to the economist. He regretted the time and effort he had put into his stint as a project manager: "I really had better things to do with my time and money," he told me.

So, when should you hire an expert? That depends both on your own expertise and that of your team members. It's really never too early to look for experts. The key is having lined them up beforehand so they can be called on when needed. When they are pressed into action, they must be aware of your priorities and dreams, so they can help you achieve them with their specialized talents.

TYPES OF EXPERTS

Though the type of expert will depend on the situation, there are a number of them you should identify now. These include the following.

ATTORNEYS

It is not unusual to have an attorney on your team of advisors, and it's prudent to include one, given all of the financial and non-financial issues at stake. If you do not have an attorney, connect with one while your executive function is still sharp. Get comfortable with that individual and his or her firm, so he or she can be ready to assist you in the future. The most effective attorneys for these purposes are often older, experienced, and good listeners. Younger attorneys are often excellent at technical detail, but they aren't necessarily as skillful as more experienced counselors. They maylack the wisdom to help you understand and accomplish your priorities as you get older.

A seventy-year-old friend and potential client came to me some years ago. He was aging and needed help figuring out the future of his business—an internal succession or sale. He had previously hired a large law firm to work with him. Over many hours (and much billing), he had received reorganization papers, shareholder agreements, and all sorts of memoranda about the regulatory documents that might relate to its sale or succession plan. "I have spent tens of thousands of dollars," he told me, "and have papers three inches high. But I have no idea what to do."

I knew I could help. He became a client, and we began a series of conversations. It came to light that he wanted to spend much more time on a charitable project that fascinated him. He had no possible successor employed in the business, and the business itself was in a "hot" field. When we finished our conversations, it was obvious he should sell. Making that decision required no paperwork. We hired a good investment banker and found some young lawyers to draft the sale contract.

After the transaction was completed, he often turned to my firm for legal advice and "wisdom."

Asking a client "What do you want?" takes some seniority. It also takes a willingness to work with the answer, even if it is different from the one the lawyer wanted to hear. Good lawyers have the experience and gravitas to do just that. At forty, that seventy-year-old friend was likely fully capable of balancing his business and charitable interests. At fifty, he was capable of deciding what should happen to his business. At seventy, the challenges were too great. He needed a trusted counselor to help him make a sound decision.

With age come many questions that require wisdom and conversation rather than technical expertise. An "expert," whether a lawyer or someone else, may be technically or academically grounded but without good counseling skills—the ability to listen to find out what the client wants and to help the client develop the plans to accomplish what the client wants. Often the best lawyer will be one who is a good counselor. This important concept can be illustrated by a friend of mine who ran a wonderful educational program.

My friend admittedly had no education credentials, but he wanted to build a board of educators, financial experts, and parents to govern it. On the advice of his "governance experts," he created an independent board. Then had the paperwork drawn up by lawyers who designed the entire governance structure, which gave the board unlimited powers. My friend named himself Director of the program. Within two years, though, the board fired him and hired a Ph.D. in education to replace him. He was without his occupation, income, and passion. He was miserable. "How could they do that to me," he asked, "after I selected them for their expertise?" Someone should have discussed the possibility that, at some point, the best interests of the program may lie in other leadership.

Another friend and client ran a different educational program she was "lifting" out of a larger institution. As we were considering the organizational structure, as her lawyer, I asked whether she wanted to create a board of experts in education and finance or to keep the program under family control. Her son worked there, and she thought his siblings could continue the program under her directorship and then ultimately his. I knew that she and her family saw the operation of the program as part of the family's long-term focus, and I knew the importance of it within their family culture. She decided to keep the program under family control; twenty-five years later it remains a family-controlled entity and very well run. That decision did not require a young, technically savvy lawyer. It took someone who could ask her what she wanted and discuss possible outcomes in detail.

PHYSICIANS

Increasingly, primary care doctors are becoming part of individuals' core support teams, because they are particularly equipped to help navigate the world of hospitals and specialized care. Talk to your physician about healthcare issues likely to arise, and then discuss those with your other support team members and helping hands. As you age, an expert doctor is essential to assessing your capabilities, whether driving, writing a will, or running a business. There are also geriatric physicians who specialize in aging. (Whenever I solicit advice from my own daughter, a pediatrician and child psychiatrist, she urges me to see a geriatrician by explaining that none of my ailments are pediatric!)

It is also crucial to let your doctors know about your living wills and powers of attorney. They need to understand your thinking, so your children or other loved ones can engage and apply that expertise to your wishes. They also need to understand that hospitals today have considerable influence in determining the course of action when you fall ill. A wise and long-trusted doctor can provide great support to your family and your team while guiding your medical care. (More on doctors and living wills in Chapter 4.)

FINANCIAL ADVISORS AND WEALTH MANAGERS

An aging client, a physician, called me to say he and his wife had fired their investment advisor and hired a new one. This news came as quite a shock: They had employed the same company for thirty years, using a single advisor the entire time. He had been loyal, and he had a sound succession plan in place, so I could not understand why they would leave him. The client explained that his wife served on a charitable board that had engaged a new—and very "sophisticated"—money manager. They were impressed by this financial "wiz's" new techniques, so they hired him for their personal wealth management as well. They believed he would help them "get real about great investments." My client told me, "He can take us into the newest and hottest investments, keeping us financially sound throughout our old age."

Unlike their former money manager, the new one had not known the clients for over thirty years. He had no idea how the couple had thought about their wealth in their forties and fifties, and he didn't take much stock in what they had to say now. Instead, he threw their money into the "latest and greatest." Within six months, they came to me to say this new wealth advisor had found them a lawyer to implement a great strategy for income tax savings. The attorney would enable them to take advantage of little-known special trusts and foundations.

The opportunities my client described were rather radical, and I doubted they would work from a tax standpoint. I also believed the proposed strategy was unlikely to accomplish their goals. However, as I tried to communicate my rationale, they explained they were moving forward with that bright young lawyer and that my services were no longer needed. As far as I know, they have proceeded as planned, and I expect they will ultimately suffer anxiety over their investments and resulting issues with the IRS.

When that physician left his investment advisor, he lost a resource he could not replace. Elderly, wealthy individuals are, more often than not, better off sticking with investment counselors who are willing to develop a long-term relationship. Continuity matters in financial affairs, particularly as you age. Moving from a portfolio of stocks and bonds—a strategy that usually works over the long term—into alternative investments may sound great but won't give you the comfort you may need. And that investment strategy may not be suitable for your stage of life.

The importance of continuity was reinforced to me after a meeting I had with a client and her long-term wealth advisor. The client had been approached by her sister's advisor, who claimed he was going to "smooth" out her investment performance through a portfolio of alternatives. The client was tempted by the new advisor and told us his firm planned to minimize volatility in her portfolio. The long-term counselor heard this, looked at our client and said, "I have known you forty years and you have never worried about volatility. Even through volatility, your portfolio has performed well over the long term. In fact, through three generations, your family's portfolio of stocks and bonds has done quite well."

That client wisely listened to her investment counselor. Her sister found that in periods of downside volatility, even her "protected" portfolio declined; and during periods of "upside" volatility her portfolio did not increase as much as the market. Our client recognized what her sister did not: that the best approach to dealing with investment counselors is to carefully choose one when you are young. A special bond is formed with an advisor who is with you during the course of a lifetime. Such a long-term relationship has value as you age.

DOMESTIC STAFF AND CAREGIVERS

In the 1930s, my grandmother hired an eighteen-year-old woman to cook and clean for her. Her friends called the woman a "maid," but my grandmother thought of her as a "friend." She taught her friend how to read and write and ultimately to drive. As my grandmother got older, she relied on the woman to help her shop, take her to doctors, and get dressed every morning. As my grandmother lost the capacity to drive, the woman became her chauffeur. As her medications became more complicated, the woman managed them, and even attended doctor's visits with her. Until my grandmother's death, this friend remained what we would today call a "caregiver." She also was almost like a daughter, and the relationship was ideal for both of them.

Household helpers can become excellent caregivers, but good ones are hard to find and keep. That said, it is certainly worth trying, regardless of cost. Not only will you have a tidy home, but that person can also spend time getting to know you. Over time that caregiver can understand your wants and needs and attend to them as you age, much like my grandmother's caregiver, who was with her until her death at age eighty.

Though professional caregivers are excellent resources, they are difficult to bring into your life when you are younger. In the prime of your life, their services are likely not needed on a regular basis, or at all. That being the case, you may not have the chance to build a relationship with a caregiver who can get to know you well. But you should look for opportunities. For example, one of my clients had a "librarian" for many years who filed her personal papers, managed her bills and kept her office in shape. As the client aged, the librarian provided more and more support.

When it was time for the librarian's retirement, the client was so dependent on her, she wasn't sure what to do. A sensitive geriatric care company was called in and helped her find a replacement "librarian." The successor's skills and experience were more in caregiving than librarian sciences. We then arranged with the retiring librarian to come in twice a week for three months to adequately "train" the new hire. This transition period allowed the two of them to maintain not just the filing and bill paying, but the other support the client needed as well. Today that successor keeps the client's calendar, arranges medical appointments, supervises medications, purchases groceries, serves as chauffeur, and provides exceptional support to allow the client to feel functional.

PASTORS, SPIRITUAL LEADERS, AND GURUS

An Indian industrialist once told me that, as a young man, his father advised him never to make business decisions without first consulting a guru. The industrialist took this advice to heart and regularly spoke with a guru, who was younger than him. He came to rely on the wise man's advice as he grew his business and built a family. "I consulted my guru whenever I was about to make an important decision," he explained to me. As the industrialist aged, his business became very large, and his son and daughter took on roles at the company. The guru helped him consider how to incorporate the children into senior management, and the guru began to attend all board meetings. When the industrialist became elderly, his children turned to the guru to help manage their father's affairs. Their father was comforted by the fact that his guru helped make decisions for himself and his children.

Another example is a Benedictine monk, a high school teacher, who taught and advised one of his students who came from a wealthy family. In time, the monk came to provide both educational and spiritual guidance for this student. In the process, he also developed a relationship with the student's family. He became pastor for the son and the parents, and even presided over the son's wedding. That monk performed all the family's religious services—from baptism to weddings to funerals—and attended all of the family celebrations. From time to time, the son had challenges dealing with his father, who he believed to be too controlling. Whenever issues arose, the son called the monk, who reached out to the father to work through these problems. As the father aged and began to lose executive function, the monk helped the family manage a variety of issues, including the father's loss of his faculties.

That monk was in fact like the guru. He knew the family well, understood the son, and understood the father.

Though pastors and other spiritual leaders are not for everyone, many people find comfort in having someone with such a background to speak with as they age. These conversations may range from religious or spiritual counsel to advice on major life and even business decisions. What you make of those relationships is up to you of course, but in most cases, if you have a long-term relationship with a minister, rabbi, priest, or other pastoral resource, it will be worth developing and maintaining throughout your life.

GERIATRIC SOCIAL WORKERS

Over the past fifty years, there have been remarkable developments in the study of geriatric social services. Early in my career, one of the local banks hired a geriatric social worker—one of the first to do so. The bank appointed her a trust officer, responsible for assisting clients with understanding the legal complexity of trust documents, investment portfolios, and taxation. That position gave her an easily understandable title and role, but her real capabilities went well beyond "trust officer."

When clients came to my office trying to choose a bank as trustee or executor, I could list pluses and minuses for each one: some had great historical investment performance; some encouraged their staff to join country clubs; some had great chefs. But only one had a geriatric social worker, and that was a key differentiator. I could explain that skillset had been invaluable in assisting clients with the many issues of old age, such as whether and how to stay in their homes, finding caregivers, and navigating the healthcare system.

As I explained the different options, most clients chose the bank with the on-staff social worker. I watched those clients as over time the geriatric social worker visited widows and widowers weekly, helping them organize and pay their bills, running errands, and ensuring that their staff were paid. She essentially became the trusted counselor and guiding hand to those whose capabilities were declining. She surveyed the house for dangers, such as loose carpets and stoves that did not turn off; kept the clients' children informed of their parents' health, safety, and daily activities; and found nursing homes and assisted living apartments for clients when necessary. In short, everything she did enabled the widows or widowers to maintain some independence and pursue their interests. Meanwhile, under her watchful eye, the widows' or widowers' children were allowed to lead their lives independently. From this "trust officer," my clients and I learned the value of trained geriatric expert advisors.

Though there are lawyers, doctors, and other experts who focus on aging individuals—all of which are incredibly valuable—none are as effective in helping an aging wealth holder on a day-to-day basis as a trained, geriatric social worker. Today, most people think of social workers as providing services to lower income individuals and families and those people who need assistance accessing public programs and governmental services. But geriatric social workers help people deal with the many challenges of old age—whether physical or mental, whether loss of mobility or loneliness—no matter their level of wealth or income. The only difference is that wealthy people can directly pay for those and related services provided by geriatric social workers, while others cannot. In short, a competent geriatric social worker can bring happiness and satisfaction to an aging client or relative.

Geriatric social workers can be invaluable to a family, advisors, caregivers, or other support team members dealing with the frustrations of helping a person with dementia. There are numerous "tricks" I have learned from social workers, including the code word discussed in Chapter 2. Most importantly though, their impartiality, expertise, and focus on support make them unlike any other team member or expert.

I received a call from a woman whose children were trying to "supervise" the management of her dementia. She said, "My children are trying to control me, and I resent it. Everyone is telling me what to do as if I don't know anything." She felt this way after a particularly frustrating session with her children and her doctor. I spoke with her trustees (not her children), and we agreed a geriatric social worker should be engaged. By doing so, the children backed off and the geriatric social worker took over, emphasizing "support" over "supervision." The children felt better knowing someone was there to assist their mother, and their mother loved the geriatric social worker. She said, "I'm so happy we hired her. She doesn't just constantly tell me *what* to do but *helps* me do what I want or need to."

Though there are people acting in this capacity without academic credentials, qualified social workers are specifically trained in this field. Hire only those social workers who have the appropriate credentials. An effective geriatric social worker should be able to observe and analyze a situation, then recommend appropriate resources, whether companions, caregivers, food providers, nursing facilities, or anything in between.

Whenever I am on an aging client's support team, I try to have a geriatric social worker available. That expertise was especially helpful in working with a wise civic lion in his nineties who was losing his reasoning ability. He sat quietly dejected, day after day, as his wife tried to interest him in conversations. His declining executive function and unhappiness left his wife unhappy herself. She just couldn't figure out how to "cheer him up." We called in a geriatric social worker who assessed the situation. She noted that the civic lion had spent a business career surrounded by people who talked to him as an intelligent adult. Those conversations ranged from baseball (he had season tickets) to music (he was on the symphony board) to education (he was on the University board), not to mention business and financial matters. Using that knowledge, the social worker started resourcing "companions"—people trained and accustomed to drawing out seniors into conversation and activity.

Quite impressively, the social worker located a retired professional baseball player who spent several hours reminiscing with the civic lion about the greatest teams and games in the history of the sport. After every visit, the civic lion's mood brightened. The social worker also had a violin student visit every week. As the violinist serenaded him, the man would smile and suggest different shading and tone. When the student left, the civic lion would often hum the music he had heard. Likewise, a retired stockbroker would come by once a week to talk about the markets and to describe certain stocks and strategies. He drew the lion into discussions about great companies, investors, and historic trends in markets. Engaging this aging titan through varied types of companionship, the social worker improved his mood and his life. He enjoyed the chance to spend time with people other than his wife and caregivers, and the visits also gave his wife some respite. Meanwhile, his renewed good mood lifted her spirits.

This same geriatric social worker made life joyful for another aging wealth holder with a passion for antique dolls and miniature toys. A widow, this woman had remained quite active into old age. She had a group of younger friends, but they saw less of her as her mental acuity faded. The social worker analyzed the situation and arranged a regular visit from a younger woman who practiced "doll therapy" for aging women. The therapist animated her weekly visits with the widow through vintage magazines, dolls, and toys. Using these as props, she encouraged conversation. She was able to focus the conversation on the objects themselves and keep the elderly woman engaged. After each visit, the widow would call her children to express her enthusiasm about the fun she had with her new friend.

In preparing for old age, I encourage clients in their sixties to identify geriatric social workers they like. The goal is to develop a relationship with a social worker, so that expert can gain an understanding of your desires and objectives as you get older. When clients hired the bank with the geriatric social worker, they could get to know that trust officer over matters not exclusively related to aging. The trust officer came to know the clients' finances, family, housekeepers, and friends, even before assuming responsibility for those relationships. The ideal is to create these bonds before aging becomes the only issue.

I introduced a geriatric social worker to a client in her seventies as a resource in managing household help—management the client had no interest in at the time. The client was active in a number of charitable activities and used her house as an "office" to store records, conduct meetings, and generally serve as the headquarters for a number of those activities. She relied on her husband's former secretary to keep everything in order, but the secretary herself was getting old and began talking about retirement.

With the help of a geriatric social worker, the client hired a graduate of the school of social work, who had excellent technology and organizational skills. That person was hired as a replacement "secretary" and was also highly qualified to take care of aging individuals. As the client aged and was less capable of managing her charitable activities and financial affairs, the assistant could take over many of those functions. Because the client was less capable of managing her personal affairs, the assistant took on a greater caregiving role. That secretary was professionally equipped to become a caregiver.

NEW RESOURCES

Nationally, an increasing number of services are focused on the challenges of aging for wealthy families. These agencies work for family offices (a firm or team of staffers dedicated to taking care of a family's finances, health, and philanthropy), financial services companies, and children of aging parents. This expanding industry is often entrepreneurial and designed to relieve children and family offices of responsibility for aging parents. An entrepreneur who is developing such a service told me, "The children are thrilled they can lead their own lives without worrying about mom or dad because we are taking care of them."

A wealthy friend of mine benefited greatly from one of these agencies to help with his elderly mother in Florida. He lives in the Midwest and had been traveling to see her once a week when the Covid pandemic hit. The agency's service provider now visits his mom and puts her on Zoom with the children and grandchildren for an hour a week. "Really, it's just as good as visiting Mom," said my friend. Still, with any new resource, carefully evaluate the provider's capability and do a background check. Some handle everything remotely and have limited access to their clients. A local resource is ideal, but many cities don't have such agencies, in which case the connection may need to be remote. No matter what kind of expert or service you decide to work with, do your research fully and early.

CONCLUSION

You and your support team will need outside experts, professionals who can deliver services or information your team cannot. Start early to develop a list of experts and resources who can assist you and your helping hands as you age. Some may actually become part of your support team while others will not. Get to know the experts early and make sure your team knows what you will be expecting of those experts. The sooner you can begin pulling in experts and giving them your input as you get older, the more effective they will be. These experts, whether on your support team or not, can help you and the team ensure that your old age can be productive and allow you to live life on your terms for years to come.

CHAPTER 4

HEALTHCARE: PLANNING FOR HEALTH CHALLENGES

An elderly husband and wife relied on a family doctor for many years, resisting living wills and durable powers of attorney. When the husband suffered a stroke, their doctor—then almost as old as the husband—spoke to the wife. The doctor had concluded the husband would not recover. As his physician and friend of many years, he also knew his patient would not want to be kept alive for an unnecessary, extended period of time. The wife was grateful for the physician's frank advice and readily agreed there should be no artificial life support. Together, the doctor and wife decided on a plan that resulted in the husband dying quietly, without many of modern medicine's possible interventions, but with the dignity he had always wanted. The wife later said, "If you have a good doctor, you don't need a living will. If you have a bad doctor, you should change doctors."

This woman's experience is a rule to live by. People run into a wide variety of situations that affect their healthcare decisions in advancing age. As they do, they need to rely on those who understand their wishes and have their best interests at heart. For example, a friend's husband had terminal lung cancer, so she enlisted hospice care to provide the at-home health services he needed. The hospice, associated with a major hospital, was modern, enlightened, and entirely inclined to make all decisions relating to the husband's health. However, my friend believed they were making some bad ones. The hospice recommended morphine injections to "smooth his road into oblivion." But even though he had weakened physically, his mind was sharp, and he valued his daily activities, no matter how limited.

When he refused the morphine, the hospice workers told him he would feel much better on the opiate. They tried to convince him his illness was muddling his decision-making. He and his wife discussed the matter. They concluded that the ability to read the morning paper and enjoy a few hours with his grandchildren from time to time was worth a bit of pain and a rougher "road into oblivion." Ultimately, they fired that hospice service and found a new doctor, a friend of theirs who was willing to make house calls. That doctor assured them both that any time the husband wanted morphine, it could be administered. If he didn't want it, then he should not feel obligated to take it. They also found a caregiver who could spend time with the husband during the day when his wife was unavailable or needed to tend to her own affairs.

As we age, we face more and more healthcare decisions. Unwelcome developments are more frequent as time wears on the body. Of course, illness can come in youth as well, but old age has a knack for finding the infirmities lurking around every corner. Each visit to the doctor and every routine check-up open the door to some hidden malady that may need attention. Weeks can be filled with doctors' appointments or medical tests. The older I get, the more I feel the need to answer the question of "How are you?" by responding, "I am fine, until someone tells me I am not!"

So, any planning for your aging must take into account the possibilities of ill health. It has already been noted that the near universal desire, "I want good health," tops our list of priorities with age. Also as noted, the statement leaves unanswered, "Good for what?" Answering that question, setting priorities, and re-affirming your passions will be key to healthcare planning. To start, let's look at some fundamentals of preparation for declining health.

PLANNING EARLY, PLANNING OFTEN

Most planning for aging starts with a "Living Will," "Durable Power of Attorney for Healthcare," or some similar expression of wishes, as we noted in Chapter 2. This delegation of responsibility governs your health in the event of partial or full incapacity. However, these often legally binding documents are rarely clear enough to cover the surprises that may come your way. Lawyers write them, and hospitals ask for them when you are admitted. Once you're there, all kinds of procedures are set in place to ensure the hospitals and doctors have no legal liability for their decisions. They rely on the documents or the persons designated under them. In essence, it's a legal automatic pilot.

These documents should always be in place, but they should never be executed without conversations and clear expression of wishes *beforehand*. It's important to note that after they are signed, they are never finished. Too many times I've seen documents that should have been updated but weren't. Regular consideration and discussion should take place right up to the time it is no longer possible. Written expressions of direction or clinical legal documents alone will not allow the layers of meaning and subtleties that can be communicated in a conversation. For these documents to work as intended, you need to sit down with your doctors, family members, and others—including lawyers, pastors, caregivers, or other experts covered in Chapter 3—to talk about possibilities and eventualities which may need to be faced in your healthcare. Your thoughts and feelings about the challenges of illness and your understanding of your doctor's perspective can help inform those conversations. It is important for the doctor to understand you, and for you to understand the doctor. And if you find that you, as the patient, and the doctor do not seem to be compatible, you need a new doctor—and the doctor needs a new patient.

Indeed, you and your doctors may not always see eye to eye on best steps forward, and the "best" medical advice is not always correct. There is no better illustration of that fact than the following story. A pediatrician told the parents of a child who was born with severe birth defects that their son would die within a year or two. The doctor explained that the child would be hard to care for, would disrupt the family's life, and would be difficult for the parents' other children to deal with. He recommended they move the child from the hospital where he was born to a home "where he could find comfort before his untimely passing." Following their doctor's advice, though they were uncomfortable doing so, the parents placed the child to a care facility and treated the child as if he had died. They decided never to visit him.

But the child's elderly grandfather was unwilling to "write off" his grandson. At his age, the grandfather concluded that he could not treat the child as if he were "dead." He visited him every week. To his surprise and delight, he saw his grandson progressing every time, supported by devoted caregivers. After three years, the grandfather insisted the child be taken out of the home and returned to the family. With the help of the caregivers, the grandfather found a pediatrician who could see that child's full capability. Today, that child is a forty-year-old functional adult fully engaged in life! And he ended up being raised in a loving family.

It's important to have necessary discussions with your doctors. It is also fundamental that they share your values and views of the world. No doctor is "always right," but if you settle for someone you fundamentally disagree with, your healthcare decisions may not turn out how you wanted, or planned for, in old age. If you have explicit conversations with your doctors, they should be able to develop a sensitivity to your beliefs, fears, expectations, and limitations. As they get to know you through conversations, your doctors should also be able to try to take the course of action that seems best for you from *your* perspective.

NECESSARY CONVERSATIONS AND DECISIONS

No matter whom you pick to administer care, so long as you are perfectly competent, *you* are the best person to decide on the medical advice and to make your healthcare decisions. These include the treatments to take and not to take, as well as the advice to seek and follow—up to a point. Determining that point, however, is not always easy. When you are unconscious, for example, you have clearly passed that point. But suppose your reasoning is challenged and you can no longer recognize your inability to make your own informed decisions. This situation happens frequently later in life. The question then becomes, who should step in, when, and how?

It is important to build relationships over time with those people on whom you would rely if you were unconscious, incapacitated, or unable to exercise sound judgment. It's better to start that collaboration before you become "unreasonable." Conversations about medical care should ideally occur when you are young, not at death's door. They should take place when you are alert, reasonably well, and view illness as a "what if" scenario. In addition to speaking with doctors, you need to have these conversations with anyone who will help you, such as the individuals you would talk with about your living will or durable power of attorney. Family, or other support team members and helping hands, should also be involved in similar discussions while you are of sound mind and body.

The conversations should take into account that illness can lead to poor decision-making. A neurologist I know says that ill patients who wish to be euthanized are simply "clinically depressed" and need treatment for their mental health. To avoid any confusion, discuss with your doctors how seriously they should take your expressions about ending your life. Meanwhile, consider your own religious beliefs or pragmatism and make those clear to your doctor as well.

If you have a good internist, a "Concierge doctor," or a relationship with a hospital, these conversations can be easily arranged. And they should be. "Concierge doctors"—doctors who, for an annual fee, are available by phone 24 hours a day—may seem a luxury. However, these doctors generally have more time for healthcare discussions. They should be willing to spend time with you and regularly talk about your potential healthcare issues with your family, your helping hands, and members of your support team.

Those conversations could possibly include not only the internist, but various specialists convened by the internist and other trusted professional advisors and experts, including lawyers, family office employees, and religious leaders. Keep in mind, many hospitals are willing to extend special services and attention to their philanthropic donors. Indeed, some hospitals have concierge doctors sent by the hospital foundation to visit with patients and arrange special services. Here, as well, your wealth may make these conversations more accessible.

Any person signing a "living will" or other end-of-life directive should spend at least fifteen minutes every year (possibly during an annual physical), with a doctor and family member discussing the implications of such a directive. That conversation should include how the outcomes of those visits are to be interpreted by doctors, hospitals, and family members, touching on specifics as much as possible. This updating process should give you peace of mind as you age. It is important to recognize that if you want responsible healthcare decisions made on your behalf, you should be willing to lose some of your independence over time. By clarifying your late life medical care preferences, you can have some confidence that your plans will be executed.

Consider discussing some of the following questions with all parties involved. Though they may not be the most pleasant conversations, they may prove essential to the health-care decisions you make, or those that need to be made for you:

- How low must the chances for recovery be when the plug is pulled?
- Are you willing to risk a chance of survival of 5 percent?
- What level of awareness would make your life worth living (for example, to see grandchildren, to watch television)?

- How will the prospect of relieving pain be balanced against the loss of acuity that may come with heavy medications, such as morphine?
- How binding should your expression of wishes really be when you can no longer truly express them?

These are just a few of the questions that need to be asked up front and then again at regular intervals.

It is crucial that the right people be at the table in these conversations, so selecting them requires careful consideration. Just as a "good doctor" needs no real written direction (assuming that the doctor has spent time understanding his or her patients) and a bad doctor needs to be fired, your selection of "attorneys in fact for healthcare," or those who will carry out your wishes, must be focused on ensuring that the appropriate person or people are chosen as decision-makers. Just as you need to carefully consider who might be appropriate as trustees, your selection of healthcare decision-makers needs to carefully consider candidates by looking at their capabilities and qualifications.

IDENTIFYING AND CHOOSING DECISION-MAKERS

Unfortunately, parents usually name all their children as attorneys-in-fact for medical care without any real concern for whose judgment would make most sense, and who might be willing to look at the parents' situation most clinically. The following story highlights the inevitable confusion that occurs when multiple decision-makers are chosen. A wealthy woman with four children was dealing with her ninety-year-old husband, who was suffering from dementia, among other medical challenges.

The woman's cognitive abilities were also declining, and consequently she was not entirely capable of making decisions. The family decided to have regular family conferences to discuss her husband's condition and treatment. Significantly, three of the children were doctors—an internist, a pediatrician, and a psychiatrist. All four children and the mother were on the durable power of attorney for healthcare, so all of them were involved in the decisions about the husband's medical care.

The first family meeting, over the dinner table, devolved into a shouting match. The four children fought over multiple questions: Who should be their father's primary doctor? What specialists did he need? Was the dementia he was experiencing really Alzheimer's or just a simple case of dehydration? The child who was not a doctor promoted the use of a traditional practitioner of eastern medicine he had found in Mexico City. With the mother in tears, the four children ultimately stormed out of the dining room. Each used his or her durable power to call a doctor (or in the case of the one son, the practitioner in Mexico).

Within a week, their father's attending doctors were left completely immobilized by the family's infighting, and new doctors were circling the patient. The father's healthcare was only resolved by his death, which left the family in a state of disharmony, even arguing over what undertaker to use and whether to cremate or bury their father. Family relationships were fractured, and the mother ultimately decided that the internist child should be her only attorney in fact for healthcare.

Another woman I know had a husband who, at a relatively young age, developed dementia. She was his second wife, and he had a son through a prior wife. The husband had been optimistic that his son and new wife would get along and develop the love between them that he had for each of them separately. So, in deciding who would take care of him in old age, he named his son *and* his wife to manage his care. Rather than growing closer over time, however, the relationship between his son and wife worsened.

As the dementia settled in, the wife used her husband's wealth, which was fairly substantial, to move him to one of the finest assisted living facilities. She was comfortable knowing he was being treated well, and he seemed to enjoy his new home. The son, on the other hand, argued that his father's money was being "wasted." He believed his father should be placed in a cheaper facility "since he won't know the difference anyway."

The son began calling his father's doctors, insisting they give him regular reports on their patient. He tried to convince them to advise his stepmother that the long-term care amenities at the facility were unnecessary, nor that they would be appreciated by his father. He also started arguing with various caregivers at the facility about the details of treatment and fighting with the management and administrators about the costs. The wife found herself trying to protect the caregivers and care facility from the son's visits. Ultimately, she began litigation to keep the son from visiting his father, and the father died before the litigation was completed. That father, of course, loved his wife and his son. But it was not reasonable to think they would work together in support of his healthcare. He needed to choose one or the other—likely his wife—to avoid such a toxic situation.

It is not unusual to see a patient on a death bed with various attorneys-in-fact consulting the doctor and coming to different conclusions. More than once, doctors have had to watch the family dynamics from the sideline, left perfectly incapable of providing. Too often, when an entire family is brought into a stressful decision-making process, rivalries and rifts in relationships that have been growing over many years resurface. Poor family dynamics can create absolute dysfunction regarding life-or-death decisions, leaving the parent effectively victimized.

CRITERIA FOR CHOOSING DECISION-MAKERS

So, how do you avoid such outcomes and wisely choose your decision-makers? A spouse alone is often a good start. If children are to serve as decision-makers, start by considering geography. The principle of proximity is important. Who is likely to be around? Then, consider their maturity level and who among your family has sound reasoning capacity. Think about whom you would truly trust to make such important decisions. The key realization is that your attorneys-in-fact for your healthcare is *not* an expression of love. As important, naming a number of family members (regardless of their reliability or capabilities to handle such decisions) is not a way to express "equal love for all." You must choose decision-makers on a pragmatic basis. Your proxy should be the person who is the most qualified, available, willing, caring, and objective. You should also consider with whom you communicate most easily and clearly and who knows you best.

The potential decision-maker's economic situation might also play a role. Who is likely to be "waiting around" for an inheritance? For example, a ninety-seven-year-old client of mine in relatively good health had three children. She was beneficiary of a trust worth $500 million dollars to be divided among those children at her death. Two of the children, her sons, were self-sufficient and actively pursuing careers. The third, her daughter, was often without cash to live on and frequently turned to her mother for help. The two self-sufficient children marveled at their mother's capability and continued strength. They were proud of her and treated her with respect and dignity. The daughter, however, said to me, "Mom is now on a walker. I cannot imagine she wants to live like that. She will deteriorate soon and quickly. Of course, I will miss her, but it will be nice to finally have my money." It was an easy decision for that ninety-seven-year-old woman—not surprisingly she did not name her daughter as her attorney-in-fact.

Dangers can also arise when you refuse to choose decision-makers or if the ones you identify are decision-makers in name only. As mentioned, though you may be the best person to manage your own healthcare for a time, you will reach a point when you must rely on others. You should not allow yourself to face old age, and its attending health issues, alone. For example, an older woman who had been widowed young raised two children on her own, both of whom relied on her financially and emotionally into their middle age. This woman had always been ready to make decisions for her family but, like so many of us, she faced medical issues as she aged. One day, she was hospitalized for a serious operation. After it had been performed, she returned home, saying she felt great. Still, her doctor advised her to retain twenty-four-hour care for several months to monitor her blood pressure and ensure that she regularly took the medication he had prescribed her.

Several days after her release, she announced she was all better and didn't need any further care. That had been her first overnight stay in a hospital, and she hated it. "The hospital was miserable, the food was horrible, and the nurses treated me like a moron," she said. "The doctors thought they knew more than

I do and wanted to tell me how to live my life. One even told me I needed a nurse at home! I am done with all that."

Meanwhile, the woman's two daughters—both of whom lived out of town and were considered her designates for her medical care—paid little attention to their mother. They assumed she was fine. They reasoned, she had always been independent and would remain independent. When a family friend and advisor suggested that they reinforce what the doctor was saying, one daughter replied, "Mother would not listen to us even if we told her what to do. Besides, mother knows how to take care of herself." Unknown to them, or anyone else, their mother was not taking her medication, was not eating, and on some level, was killing herself. She died alone in her apartment two weeks after returning from the hospital. Her care was relegated to the undertaker rather than the medical industry.

Sadly, this woman was not capable of making her own medical decisions or caring for herself, even though she asserted she was, and appeared to be, competent. Her daughters, to whom she had assigned responsibility for her medical care, were unwilling to consider she might need help and might not be able to think clearly. Her strength of character—one that had been central to their family—kept the two of them from helping her make the appropriate decisions to keep her healthy and safe. She should have found delegates who might not consider her so overpowering and would have been willing to exercise control.

This story raises another critical point about choosing your decision-makers: Your attorneys-in-fact need to have the ability and authority to tell you that they know better than you when the time comes. They must have the confidence and wherewithal to determine the medical care necessary when they sense your reasoning ability is diminished. Often, that person will be a daughter or son who works closely with a doctor. That child can, in fact, consistently serve as a medical intermediary during your lifetime. (As mentioned, I'm fortunate to have a child who is a doctor. A number of times I have asked one of my own doctors to review his or her findings with my daughter—even when I am perfectly capable of understanding them.) A spouse, child, or caregiver can also attend your doctor's appointments to evaluate your understanding and reasoning. If that's been the practice over years, you will become accustomed to sharing medical information and your aches and pains with your helping hand. The person accompanying you will then be better prepared to play a role in your care.

CONSEQUENCES OF THE WRONG CHOICE

If you have multiple attorneys-in-fact and they cannot agree, then what happens? This can occur when you require immediate health-related decisions, such as life support intervention. As mentioned, disagreement is likely to confuse the doctors and hospital. You can end up in limbo or receive standard treatments you may not actually want. In essence, that means one of the quarreling parties wins simply by quarreling. There are an untold number of stories of patients left on life support for years in the wake of an initial argument about whether to put them on at all.

When immediate decisions are not required, the quarrel becomes the family fight, as we've seen earlier in the chapter with the four children pitted against one another. Or, in the case of the wife and stepson, the fight became a court battle, with hundreds of thousands of dollars spent in attorney's fees.

Neither is helpful or pretty. An objective observer would find it difficult—if not impossible—to see love and care for the patient "at the center" of the battle. Further, the doctors you will need when facing serious illness are rarely equipped to handle family arguments. Unfortunately, these medical professionals are often caught in the middle of such feuds. The doctors who received calls from the stepson making demands for information and control over the father's treatment turned to the wife to figure out what to do. Still, that also put the doctors in a position of possibly being sued by the son, as well as by his stepmother. How difficult for doctors to give good medical treatment and advice in these situations!

Indeed, these battles make family fights over money look relatively minor. In practice, courts and lawyers are more structurally equipped to handle family financial disagreements than medical ones. After all, financial disputes can often be resolved by application of fiduciary rules or state statutes. Medical disagreements are difficult to resolve when those involved are all given equal authority by governing documents. For these reasons, selecting your healthcare decision-makers can be more important than choosing the trustees who handle your money and wealth. Trustees can be professionals unrelated to the settlor or beneficiaries. And most professionals would resist accepting responsibility for medical care and medical decisions.

To compare the ease of settling financial disagreements to the challenges of settling medical disagreements, consider the following. There was a family in which a son and mother were co-trustees of a family trust. The son's sister, a spendthrift, sued both her mother and brother in an effort to have them set aside a trust the deceased patriarch had created for his daughter. Although the mother and son were opposed to setting that trust aside, they and their attorneys entered into settlement negotiations with the daughter. They settled her challenge by reforming the trust to give her its income and a power of withdrawal. The agreement was negotiated, signed, sealed, and delivered within six months of the suit's filing. The process was not pleasant, but it was based on both sides' analysis of law and facts and the evaluation of the likelihood of success. From that standpoint, it was easy compared to the health issue that developed during the negotiations.

During those trust negotiations, the mother developed severe dementia. Her doctors said that she should forego all alcohol, in part because she kept losing track of how many drinks she had during her "cocktail hour." In losing count, she also lost her balance and logic every night. The doctors said she was at risk of falling and that the heavy alcohol use was likely to aggravate her dementia. They recommended she quit drinking all together.

The son prepared to follow the doctor's orders by removing all of the liquor from the house. Meanwhile, the daughter announced that liquor was good for her mother as it gave her pleasure in life. "That doctor doesn't understand" was the daughter's viewpoint. As the son removed the liquor, the daughter arrived with new bottles and encouraged her mother to continue with her evening cocktails. This continued until the mother fell and broke her hip, then spent three months in a rehabilitation facility. Only then was the daughter willing to support the removal of liquor from the house. There could have been no reasonable basis or analysis to allow settlement of that disagreement—and there was no way to compromise on health.

Whether you are wealthy or not, the challenges in choosing decision-makers are the same, but family dynamics are often amplified when significant wealth is at stake. While it is somewhat sad to consider, some offspring of wealthy individuals may eagerly await a chance to pull the plug and get their inheritance. Disputes over treatment can be manifestations of years of simmering jealousies in which the overriding message was that love and money were central to the family's existence. Money can aggravate family relationships, and illness can often compound the fight over wealth and love.

The considerations regarding wealth management can distract from considerations of healthcare decision-making. So, the more money you have, the more time and attention you will likely spend addressing the complexities of wealth— family offices, trusts, tax planning, partnerships, and so on and so forth. Money matters are much more attractive to discuss than healthcare because they can represent the "noble" purpose of maintaining family wealth and legacy. It is much easier for financial advisors, lawyers, and accountants to discuss and build structures to provide for your financial affairs than for your medical care.

However, healthcare issues are just as important as—if not more important than—financial affairs. Particularly if you have substantial wealth, your financial matters can overshadow your medical care. It is important to recognize that management of your health is always more complex and more consequential than management of your wealth, so plan accordingly.

CONCLUSION

Even after years of careful diet, exercise, regular medical visits, and attention to health, aches and pains, illnesses sneak in. Our control over our own health visibly erodes as we age. And death by its nature—even with all the planning possible—is the ultimate loss of control. This inevitability is why it is so important to answer questions about the medical care you'd like to receive under specific circumstances and your preferred approach to healthcare before you lose control of your body or mind. Regular conversations with the people who will be supporting you are paramount. Choosing the right decision-makers will make all the difference in late-life, and end of life healthcare.

CHAPTER 5

RESIDENCE: MOVING OR STAYING PUT

When my parents were in their early sixties, they decided they had no further need for a large house "now that the children are gone." They realized their current residence was really more of a "family" home, not "the nest" my mother wanted just for the two of them. My father explained, "I want something that can be 'ours' when one of us is no longer alive. We don't want the survivor to have make a new 'home,' leaving behind the memories and comfort we built together." They consciously wanted to create a new home that could still be thought of as *their* home even after the first of them died.

So, they left their house of thirty years and moved to a co-op apartment. Together, and with great care, they fully renovated it. It quickly became their home and remained so for the next fifteen years while my father was still alive. And, for my mother, it continued to be "theirs" for the twenty years after my father had died. The apartment was entirely suitable for an aging person: no stairs, no gardening, and no outside mainte-nance. It was close to grocery stores and drug stores, as well as my parents' doctors. The building was also within walking distance of restaurants, shops, and movies. Their decision to plan early saved them from dealing with the burdens they would have encountered later on maintaining a large home or moving at an old age.

"Where will I live?" is a critical question almost every aging person faces. It is one that needs to be carefully considered. Of course, the perfect living situation varies by person, depending on their preferences and plans. So, the key issue to evaluate is, "How can I be sure my current residence allows me to lead the life I want as I get older?" Where you will live cannot be fully answered until you know *how* you want to live.

A myriad of questions will naturally run through your mind in regard to your residence, but until you set your priorities, they will be left jumbled and unanswered. These include:

- Must I move when I am old?
- If so, where shall I move?
- Can I, or should I, live alone?
- How do I manage the household?
- Should I move to live near my children?
- What do I do with all this clutter if I decide to move?

These are all important questions to address, but you can only answer them once you have decided what matters most to you. When you have, you can design your living situation to help you live as you would like to live. Of course, attitudes can change over time. What seems perfect to you when you are young, engaged, and surrounded by friends may not seem reasonable when you are old, inactive, and most of your friends have predeceased you. But it all starts with deciding what you really want in old age.

WHAT YOU WANT

So, first thing's first: What do you want? That surprisingly difficult question is all too often answered in the negative—what you *do not* want. It's common to hear people say:

- "I *do not want* to leave my house because I love it and feel sentimental about it."
- "I *do not want* to deal with the clutter; I am too busy to think about it now."
- "I *do not want* to be bothered with the hard work of moving."
- "I *do not want* to live in a nursing home."

These responses often reflect fear about making any decision. And the older you become, the harder these issues become. You are unlikely to get less busy with age. Nor does clutter get easier to manage as you age. Meanwhile, sentimentality does not put a new roof on the house when it leaks. Saying you don't want to do certain things is not a plan. The better approach is determining what you actually want and then conceiving the plan to make it happen.

In making this decision, keep in mind that a specific "piece of real estate" should not be the ultimate goal. Yes, staying in the family house forever may help you get *what* you want, but it should not be considered the end goal. The artist from Chapter 1 who loved painting in her basement, using an elevator to get to and from her studio, wanted to keep the family house to pursue her creative endeavors. The great collector we also met in Chapter 1 did not remain in his house simply to stay there; the house allowed him to continue collecting, writing, and enjoying his past.

On the other hand, a scholar I know moved *out* of his large house and into an apartment with his wife—in fact, *two* apartments in the same building. Their house was no longer practical, but the scholar had an enormous book collection that was his passion. He spent most of every day surrounded by and studying those books. Concluding that the one apartment could not host his library and study and his living quarters, he leased the adjoining apartment. There he could study quietly and without interference. That worked well for both of them. They, just as the other wealth holders mentioned, understood their priorities. The real estate was really a way to facilitate those goals. Smartly, they planned ahead by answering the fundamental question: "What is this home for?" It was to be a place to sleep, to eat, to live, and to study quietly and without interruption.

ANALYZING YOUR SITUATION

You must strategically design your environment so it works for you. Often, there is no practical need to stay in the house you lived in when you were younger. Just as you wanted a certain type of house to raise your family, you will likely have some specific needs when you are aged. When you are young enough to consider why you *don't* want to move, you should articulate the reasons. For example, it is quite useful for a couple in their early fifties to recognize the advantages of their house, so they can determine later on when those benefits become less important. This "scorecard" will be a useful guide in deciding when, or if, to move. Forward-thinking analysis is the basis for a conscious, informed, and definitive decision.

I went through such an analysis with a sixty-year-old couple living in a large house in a big city. Their building was enormous, consisting of three stories, and was expensive to heat, cool, and maintain. The couple listed what they liked about the house:

- The house had fond memories.
- They liked having a garden.
- Their grandchildren enjoyed spending the night when they were babysitting.
- The house was full of "stuff" they didn't want to go through.

After they drew up the list, we examined it together. Fond memories are nice, but a person can become a prisoner of memories. This point calls to mind the Dickensian character Miss Havisham, the eccentric spinster who clung to a house of nothing but memories. That's no way to live out your years.

Gardens are available on terraces or communally in an apartment building. These shared spaces also have the advantage that if you don't want to pull weeds, someone can pull them for you. An apartment or smaller house can have room for grandchildren, who in any event might have fun staying with you in a hotel on the money you save by not running a big home.

As for "stuff," we often find a house literally decaying around an elderly occupant. As old age advances, all of your items (whether considered trash or treasure) do not get easier to manage, organize, or dispose of. Papers or souvenirs you could easily find at forty may be difficult to locate at seventy— after three more decades of accumulating stuff. When you are young and alert, you will know who is in the old photographs, where you found that trinket, or why a piece of jewelry would have sentimental value to someone. As you age, all of these details may fade. If you and a spouse are having trouble figuring out how to rid yourself of "stuff," imagine how much harder it will be for the surviving spouse or, worse, for your children or grandchildren.

We discussed all these points with the couple. Though the conversation about whether their "stuff" should keep them in place was difficult and heated, they eventually sold the big house and disposed of the "stuff." They moved into a one-story home in a nice neighborhood in the suburbs. There, they felt they could live comfortably and safely for many years. They built new memories, set up a small garden, and still enjoyed sleepovers with their grandchildren, who loved the new home and were happy for their grandparents. As for the "stuff," they didn't miss any of it.

OVERCOMING SENTIMENTALITY

When it comes to living arrangements for aging wealth holders, unhappy endings are often the result of paralyzing sentimentality. For example, one woman I knew lived in what had been a lovely wooden suburban house built by her father some eighty years earlier. She had grown up there, sharing it with her father until his death. While he was alive, he maintained the home, repairing and refinishing whatever was needed. But after he died, the daughter was unable to do so. She lived in it without regard to its condition. Gradually, it began to fall apart. She would place a bucket under a leaking roof. A wedge was used to hold a door closed. She tolerated cold water from a faulty faucet in the bathroom. A termite infestation literally started hollowing out the rooms. Field mice ran freely across the floors.

Nevertheless, she didn't seem to notice or mind. She loved the house and was unwilling to leave. Yet, she was forced out when the county inspector condemned the place. He demanded a top-to-bottom renovation, but she refused. "My father built this house and said it would be solid forever," she argued. "I refuse to kill its character by renovating it." With help, she eventually found a small room in an assisted living program. Heartbroken and separated from her and her father's house, she died within six months. A sorrowful story, indeed.

Another tale of woe had similar contours. A single, older woman lived in a turn-of-the-century house, which had been built for her parents as a wedding gift from her grandfather. It was a grand structure, beautifully constructed, and reputed to have cost $1 million in 1906—about $28 million in 2020 dollars. She had been a socialite of the highest order, often entertaining in that house, and coming to feel as if it were part of her. It held a great deal of family history as well. Unfortunately, as she aged, she became more and more reclusive. Her final ten years were spent alone, unseen by anyone except the housekeeper, who came four or five days a week.

The house had been the center of the woman's life, but its purpose was no longer clear. It provided a roof over her head, but more than anything else, it fed her sentimentality. With age, she grew eccentric and rash. She never married or had children, and she was determined that no one else should ever live in the house after her death. Her will stipulated that the home be demolished once she was gone. She died in the house, alone, surrounded by closets brimming with sterling, china, and memorabilia from eras long past. That house was full of sentimentality, yes, but long stale and divorced from any human connection. The neighbors had no such attachment to the house, but they considered it a beautiful, important feature of the neighborhood. They went to court to stop the demolition and won their case. New owners renovated from top to bottom and tossed the sterling, china, and ancient mementos. They also happily raised a family there.

Homes can easily decay when the owner is consumed by sentimentality. Houses need new memories for fresh meaning from time to time. A large "family" house with one elderly occupant is often a sad place. A large house with a noisy, loving family, however, is wonderful, as new memories are constantly being created. In a way, it is unfair to let such a house fall apart simply because the owners want to preserve cherished memories. Further, "sentimentality" is quite often just an excuse for an aging homeowner's inertia or refusal to deal with the effort of moving. Most people agree they do not want a fraying house, a sad unused home, or a ghostly shrine to times gone by. Which brings us back to the central question: What *do* you want? Saying you want a home because it is full of memories may be easier and less emotionally taxing than coming up with a well-conceived and honest answer. But an answer is necessary.

CONSIDERING GEOGRAPHY

Geography may play a role in determining where you want to live. If you don't plan ahead, who will decide whether and where you move? In what city you will live when you are no longer capable of making that decision? Do you want your children to unilaterally decide you are moving near one of them, uprooting you from your comfortable surroundings? Without a plan that everyone understands, unpleasant surprises await the aging wealth holder.

The reality is that many aging people have children who live out of town. Sometimes, several children live in cities far from each other and their parents. And their location greatly affects where their parents may decide to live. It may be easier if you have one child or several children in one city. But suppose you have two children in different cities? Do you want to move from city to city every year—say six months in Boston and six months in San Francisco—to accommodate them? Your children may even end up arguing over where it's best for you to go, when, and how. Your decisiveness, however, can head off such disagreements among your children.

Though it might be nice to live near children and grandchildren, you might consider how your presence will fit into their lives and how it will affect yours. Suppose you plan to remain engaged in social activities in your home city or you have a great group of friends and support in your community. If you move just to be closer to family, you may wind up missing your friends and normal routines and feel alienated. On the other hand, if the community you now live in has no easy transportation options, as you age, will you be able to access all the benefits you currently enjoy there? And if you have a partner who passes away, no family nearby, and no way to get around, living alone would be vastly more difficult.

There are many people who move to Florida or Arizona and return home for several months every year, typically in the warmer months, to spend time in a social whirl with all their old friends. This "snowbird" lifestyle may sound ideal, but there are potential difficulties as well. For example, during the early days of the pandemic, many such people were frozen (or baked) in place in Florida or Arizona. Though a unique situation, at this point, no one knows how long Covid will be with us. Further, who's to say we might not experience a similar situation in years to come? This could make travel almost impossible, even if the back and forth is between homes of various children.

One of my clients was born and raised in a midwestern city. As a young widow, she brought up her two daughters there, both of whom moved to different places on the east coast when they grew up. The widow regularly visited them and their families when it was still easy for her to travel. As she aged, she was surrounded by friends and seen as a prominent member in her community. Each of her daughters wanted her to arrange for assisted living in her own city, but their mother would never consider leaving town to live with one of her daughters. "Why would I move somewhere where I don't know anyone?" she asked.

That widow wisely and strategically kept herself active as she aged. She made a number of younger friends who continued to visit her even as her mobility declined. She also designed an entire philanthropic giving program to ensure continued attention and visits from directors of museums and other institutions. She died in her beloved community and never had to move to a foreign city.

Another aging mother loved her house, which she and her architect husband had designed and built together some twenty years before he died. Her husband had been a collector of architectural details from old houses in the neighborhood—cornices, fireplaces, tiles, cast iron, and old bricks. Their home was a masterpiece, and importantly, it had been designed so they could stay in it for many years. It was one story, with plenty of space for household help, easily accessible bathrooms, and other details that suited them. There was no question she could comfortably stay in that house after his death, and she wanted to.

Yet both her children lived in another city three hours away by car. They wanted her to live near them and her grandchildren.

In this instance, the woman was willing to leave her location but not her house. With the support of her children, she "moved" the house by building the identical structure in her children's neighborhood. With her enormous wealth, she had the architectural detail work transferred from her old house to the new one, piece by piece. And there she lived happily until she died. A unique approach? Most definitely. Extreme? Maybe. But when it comes to your residence—like many other aspects of aging—great wealth can be deployed to achieve your specific goal, whatever that may be. So, consider the possibilities your wealth can offer. Never miss opportunities to take advantage of it to live the most fulfilling life possible.

BUILDING YOUR PLAN

If you *really* want to remain in your house, first conduct a thorough analysis of the advantages and disadvantages. If the benefits truly outweigh the burdens, you will need a plan to address the burdens. The drawbacks may include loneliness, the challenges of living twenty-four-hours-a-day with a caregiver, the possibilities of theft, and numerous questions about safety and independence. As with so many other issues for the aging wealth holder, these assessments need to be done when you are still capable of discussing them reasonably with your children or your support team. They need to understand your plans and the reasoning behind those plans. To help them, create hypothetical scenarios and benchmarks that will give them crucial information to ensure your wishes are followed.

There is no question that maintaining a sprawling family residence can be a burden. Moving out of a big house can provide the freedom to chase your dream as you age. But there are also situations in which real estate can actually *create* a mission of self-actualization. The very act of building your residence can be part of how you chase your dream. In that case, the burden may be worth it, as it was for a successful developer I knew. For many years, he and his wife lived in their house in a nice neighborhood, happily raising their family there. But in their sixties, they decided they wanted to move to an apartment for convenience, one that would suit them in the future. However, the developer was a perfectionist. The city's apartment inventory was old and run down, and he felt no building fit their needs. As a developer, his solution was obvious: Build one.

Surveying apartments throughout the country, he was intent on finding exactly what he was looking for—a building with big windows, unobstructed views, and nearby shopping and restaurants. He also wanted friends as neighbors. His search turned up a location overlooking a large park, and he designed a twenty-story building for the site. After conceiving his apartment exactly as he wanted it, he made a standing offer to his older friends: Any of them could purchase a unit before construction. Each of the buyers could the customize the apartment entirely to their own tastes. Every unit would have big windows with commanding vistas. To ensure the southern view of the building would never be obstructed, he also bought another lot to the south of the building. He chose that side for his own apartment.

When the building was completed, most of the units were occupied by people who had been his friends. Because he built it so well, they remained his friends afterwards! The developer lived in his building well into his eighties through the death of his first wife. His health being excellent, he then re-married. His new wife owned a small house, and she insisted he move into it to make it "their" house. For the rest of his life (he died at 105), he regularly visited his building, introducing any new resident to the building's history and sharing the story of its construction. He maintained his love for the building right up to his death.

Masterfully, the developer created a thoughtful strategy for aging. It not only provided for his own residence, but also allowed him to stay involved in his passions—architectural design and construction—long after he left the day-to-day business. He improved his life as he aged and also that of his friends who moved into the building. It allowed him to be neighbors with the people he enjoyed. Though many would have considered this option a burden, that building became the culmination of a career and lifestyle. The lesson is clear: Move when you are young enough. Have a plan and make your new residence a true home for you and your spouse or your partner. And if that new residence is an outlet for your mission or goal, so much the better.

ASSISTED LIVING FACILITIES

The easy plan, though not always the best plan, is to relocate to an assisted living residence with graduated levels of care. You move in when you are seventy and live in your own apartment with a kitchen, accessible dining facilities, and lots of friends. When you need full-time care, you transition to a one-bedroom with more assistance. And when you reach a stage of dementia, you get moved to a memory care floor with twenty-four-hour nursing. That all sounds well organized, even if not particularly appealing. With enough money, you can live in a facility that provides for lots of companionship, luxury spaces, entertainment, and full services as needed.

Care facilities may be an easy strategy, but many aging wealth holders find them unappealing. The prospect of living in an "oldsters" community lacking the energy common in vibrant surroundings can feel like being let out to pasture. The retirement communities of Florida or Arizona are easy, but not everyone's cup of tea. If you have not planned well, however, they are likely to be your default. In truth, care facilities can be part of a plan, but they should not be the *entire* plan.

A friend who was aging well arranged for his wife to move into a facility specially designed for people with dementia. He was in his early eighties and some of his friends urged him to move to the same facility into a building next door to hers. "You can walk to see her every day," they told him. In reality, he didn't want to "walk to see her every day"—he far preferred driving a bright red sportscar with the top down. Instead, he sold his house and moved into an apartment for students and young professionals. He was given a special parking spot, drove himself to work every morning, and made many friends among his new neighbors. They wined and dined him, and he reciprocated, enjoying their company. And he drove his car to visit his wife every day.

At the age of ninety-two, walking began to grow painful. He told me, "It is now time for a slight change in lifestyle. I have arranged to move to a facility where they will feed me when I don't feel like cooking and drive me to work if I have trouble walking to the car." During the early months of the Covid-19 pandemic, food was made for him for every meal. He had a nice porch off his apartment, telephoned his wife every day—no visitors were allowed at her place at the time—and maintained the most optimistic disposition imaginable. His last months were happily spent in that new home, which from his perspective he had moved to at just the right time.

Staying in your house or apartment will avoid an assisted living facility and retain your independence. However, staying in your residence may also deprive you of the companionship common in such a facility. Many aging people deliberately choose these facilities for the comradery and social interaction. Even then, there are trade-offs. A friend of mine encountered the companionship anathema this way: "I like young people, not old people." She refused to visit friends in homes for the elderly. "I will never enter an old folks' home," she said.

But solitary living, whether in a house or an apartment, can be quite lonely. As she aged, the woman was confronted with the reality that more and more of her friends were dying or disappearing into nursing homes. She had fewer visitors as she became less mobile. She was fortunate to have a few young friends who called on her and family who included her in dinners and other social events. But most of her meals were spent alone as she was unable to find company. She may have, in fact, been better off with the companionship of other "old folks" in an assisted living arrangement.

One woman I knew with great wealth planned for her own long-term assisted care in an unusual, but quite effective way. In her mid-nineties, she began contemplating whether or not to stay in her house, a beautiful old place in which she employed a number of loyal housekeepers, including a cook and a chauffeur. She decided to essentially "test out" assisted living. Every summer for three weeks, she gave her staff a vacation, closed the house, and moved into a nursing home. Though a generous way for her staff to coordinate their time off, more importantly, this arrangement brought the woman peace of mind.

"I want to reinforce my decision not to move to a facility," she said. "I also want the reassurance that if I lose my help, I could tolerate a such a place. This knowledge allows me to sleep well every night." That woman was blessed. She spent three weeks a summer in a facility every year, never omitting her annual "nursing home vacation." At well past 100, she died in her house in her sleep surrounded by her loyal staff.

One important note on nursing homes and assisted care facilities: the Covid-19 pandemic has forced some reevaluation of these facilities. Even those people who saw them as a reasonable place for old age and a "good place for my parents" should be having second thoughts. These homes have often gotten locked down during virus outbreaks and banned visitors. Going forward, your selection criteria must focus on hygiene and safety. If this ends up being your chosen option, talk to the facilities beforehand to understand their protocol for a similar situation in the future.

AT-HOME CARE

If you are uninterested in living in an assisted care facility, your safety and well-being may require twenty-four-hour caregivers at your home. Your planning should consider whether and how you would deal with that round-the-clock "companion." One of the advantages of wealth is that you can likely afford this level of care. But that physical comfort and care may only go so far—you may find your "intellectual care" lacking depending on your caregiver. No matter how kind and well-intentioned your caregiver may be, his or her companionship may not be the most stimulating. Caregivers do not come with the trappings of family dynamics (though in some cases that may be a good thing). How your personalities mesh or clash will play a major role. What's more, the existence of the caregiver may initiate a struggle for independence that leads to unhappiness for both you and your support team.

Many aging individuals who reluctantly agree to continuous in-home care end up fighting with their providers. Elderly employers often try to fire their caregivers—despite all of the careful interviewing and vetting done by their children or professionals. Aging wealth holders, especially those who are starting to lose their cognitive abilities, often convince themselves that they cannot get along with their caregivers. When told that the caregivers should not, or cannot, be fired, the aging wealth holder can become even more resentful. We've seen some act so rudely that it is unbearable for the caregivers. In such cases, the caregivers may simply resign.

We had one client go through two or three caregivers *a week*. She fired each until her children hired an army of twenty caregivers to rotate. The mother's dementia was such that her children let her fire anyone she wanted, but they would then recycle the fired caregiver every two or three days. The mother never realized the person arriving Thursday morning was the "incompetent" she had fired on Tuesday afternoon.

Another aging client in need of care developed a strategy of engaging and grooming a tolerable caregiver who would live in her large house. When the client had been in her fifties, she hired a young housekeeper whom she treated as a daughter. The housekeeper's salary was generous. She also provided the woman with a car and paid her daughter's school tuition. The housekeeper was entirely devoted to our client. As our client aged, the housekeeper easily and happily evolved into a caregiver role. When the client was in her mid-eighties, and dementia had set in, the caregiver continued to support her. The caregiver also hired additional help to run the household, and eventually managed a full team. Throughout that time, she lovingly took care of the client every day, and despite the dementia, the two of them stayed close.

In considering at-home care, an ever-present concern of children and surrogates is the possibility of theft. Generally, older individuals may be more likely to become the target of theft, but the possibility seems particularly acute when a caregiver is involved. Caregivers may regularly be alone in the house with their clients, meaning they have the opportunity to take advantage of the situation, pocketing a trinket or valuable that would be nice to own. But quite often, as dementia sets in and a person cannot find a favorite ring or a valuable pendant, it is always murky whether the item has been misplaced or actually stolen.

An older man complained to his children that a bar of gold, which he had been keeping for financial security, had been stolen by his chauffeur. The children thought it was unlikely; the chauffeur had been employed by their father and his company for many years. Nevertheless, the old man called the police and reported the theft, then fired the chauffeur to everyone's dismay. After the old man's death, the gold bar was found at the bottom of a freezer, where he must have hidden it for safekeeping and forgotten it was there.

Indeed, it is not unusual for an aging person to hide objects to guard against theft and then assert nefarious intent when he or she cannot remember where it was hidden. So, if you plan to stay in your house, consider putting a system in place so you don't wind up accusing loyal staff and caregivers of crimes they have not committed. Still, though it's important to assume everyone's best intentions, keep in mind that theft is possible. Depending on the size and quality of your staff, you may have to endure some thievery. If you're concerned, place valuables in a safe deposit box or outside the house altogether.

DECIDING TO STAY PUT

If you are determined to stay in your current residence—and especially if it is a large home— two critical, practical questions must be answered. First, who will be responsible for maintaining the home when you are not? Second, in what condition do you want the home to be kept and what improvements would you want made? The woman who lived in her father's house in the country until it was condemned did so without doing anything to it at all. She did have a "caretaker" who watered the lawn and swept the steps from time to time. Unfortunately, he knew nothing of maintaining a roof or the integrity of electrical wiring. And even if he had, he would have had no idea of his mandate or authority.

There need to be explicit instructions regarding who is responsible for the upkeep of your home and appropriate improvements. Those decisions may be left to your helping hands, but they will have to rely on experts for their help. So, whoever is going to be responsible for your residence needs to understand the standard of care and overall maintenance you will expect. To help, discuss and answer the following questions with them:

- What standards of cleanliness need to be followed?
- What quality of improvements should be made?
- Should there be regular and thorough housekeeping?

- If a refrigerator or other major appliance wears out, should the replacement be of similar or lesser quality? Greater?
- Should a slate roof be repaired with slate? What's the alternative?
- Should wool carpets be replaced with wool? If not, what kind might you want?

A client who prided himself on the stellar condition of his home prepared a list of contractors and suppliers he had used over the years. They knew him and had helped him maintain his house, which was located in an upscale neighborhood. They were true experts and as a result, some of the most expensive skilled craft persons in the business. But they thoroughly understood his high standards, and he believed they were well worth the price.

He drafted written instructions that directed his trustees to use this network of workers regardless of cost. As he aged and became less capable of managing the house, his trustee—his elder son—knew to use those contractors. His daughter, not a trustee, thought the contractors' prices were too high and corners could be cut, but the son followed the instructions. The client lived out his remaining days in a house that reflected the meticulous standards he had applied throughout his lifetime.

Retrofitting a house is indeed one option to ensure that it will be manageable in old age. It is easiest when you oversee the work at a young-enough age, dealing with contractors and making decisions relating to improvements. A friend of mine told me a story about his parents who had a nice, big three-story house that he and his brothers and sisters grew up in. Everyone loved the home, and his parents were determined never to move out. When his parents were in their late sixties, they added a ground floor wing off the kitchen with a large bedroom, lots of closets, and two big bathrooms. Altogether, the living quarters in that wing were much more deluxe than those in the original house.

Now in their late eighties, my friend's parents spend all of their time in that wing and the kitchen, hardly ever using the rooms in the "old house" other than for guests. My friend says he and his siblings thought their parents were "crazy" when they added the wing. Now the family realizes that the wing itself has allowed the couple to grow old "living in their house." By starting these improvements when they were young enough to oversee them, it made it easier for them to design exactly what they knew would work.

I knew an aging novelist who, like Joyce Carol Oates, had different venues for different kinds of writing. Book reviews were written on the dining room table, essays in a sunroom, and novels in an attic. As the author aged, the attic became less and less accessible as he had trouble climbing stairs. Yet, he claimed to be "too old" to learn to pen novels in his kitchen or sunroom. He told his literary agent, "I cannot climb the stairs to the attic, and the attic is the only place I can write a novel." But his novels were good—and lucrative—the agent insisted, and he told him he should keep at it.

"I don't see how," said the author, "unless we set up a pulley system to get me up there . . . or install an elevator."

"Say no more," said the agent. The agent took on the project, calling the novelist's trustees and having them commit the funds for an elevator. This arrangement allowed him to keep writing novels and chasing his dreams (and it ensured the agent a steady stream of revenue as well). Every day, the writer took that elevator up to the attic, where he ultimately completed some of the best work of his career.

The novelist was fortunate in that he had an agent who shared the business interest in his writing. If your house must be retrofitted and you have no business partner invested in seeing improvements, what happens when you lose the capacity to deal with architects, construction contractors, and others? As you age in your house, those whom you have chosen to care for you may be faced with deciding whether to move you out or redesign the home. Redesign may require the ground floor add-on, an elevator, special fixtures, and even separate living quarters for caregivers. It may be fine to remain in the house, but you also must specify and provide for substantial improvements and capital expenditures.

CONCLUSION

Whether you live in a house for many years or have moved more recently, it's critical to develop strategies and plans about your residence as you age. My parents did that and so did the developer who built a cooperative for himself and his friends. The collector, the painter, and the novelist strategized and made plans they followed as well. The scholar with two apartments did so too. These types of plans work, but they need consideration and design before you are too old. Ask yourself, what do you want of a residence, how do you want to use it, and how can it help you be what you want to be as you age? These matters require planning and discussion with those who can help you implement a plan that will work for you in old age. Without planning, the default is a nursing home, in which case some people may thrive, while others may be far from happy. Take time to analyze what you truly want out of your home, and to what end. If you decide to move, do so when you are young enough and make your new residence a true home for you and your spouse or your partner, filling it with new memories for years to come.

CHAPTER 6
PARTNERS: LOVING IN LATE LIFE

Soon after the death of her seventy-year-old husband, a wealthy widow realized she wanted companionship going forward. So, she went out on a few dates and met a fine older gentleman about her age. They immediately connected. Though he never formally moved in with her, he spent a great amount of time at her apartment. She was happy for the company, and her children were glad that she had the company. Several years into the relationship, the widow noticed her companion was drinking heavily. At first, he seemed to hold his liquor just fine, but over the years he worsened. Maybe it was his age, or maybe he was just drinking more. In time, though, it was obvious he had become a full-blown alcoholic. Meanwhile, the widow started to lose her cognitive capabilities, and she did not seem to notice her partner was now drunk much of the day.

By that point, her caregivers—who had been coming for some time to take care of the widow—found themselves taking care of her drunken partner as well. Increasingly, the caregivers were losing patience with his behavior, and finding themselves taking care of two for the price of one, the caretakers started resenting their work. They eventually told the woman's children that if the man stayed in the apartment, they would have to quit.

The women's children were concerned about the prospect of losing the caregivers, whose services they valued. So, they contacted her partner's children to say that the matter had to be resolved. It was clear he needed twenty-four-hour care, and their mother's caregivers were no longer willing to handle him. Her children told his children that he needed to hire a caregiver of his own.

His children refused. "Your mother already has someone there to help them. Why pay someone else?" they said. Further, they didn't want to draw down their father's life savings, which would be passed on to them. "He doesn't want to spend it on your mother anyhow," his children told the widow's children.

Not surprisingly, her children were not pleased with the response. They felt the man, and his children, were taking advantage of their mother's wealth and good will. They also worried about their mother's safety and were concerned that her partner needed even more care than her. He had recently taken to falling asleep with a cigarette in his hand, passing out drunk in the building's parking lot, and driving his car into those of other residents of the building. Her friends and neighbors of many years began to worry as well, not only for her safety, but also for their own. The building manager called the widow's children to say that the two would have to leave the building unless his behavior improved.

Luckily, this woman had sat down with her children years earlier and told them her first priority was to stay in her home. Her children understood that "no matter what" happened, their mother would remain in that apartment. Because of the clarity of her priorities, the children concluded that her partner had to go. They told him and his family he could no longer remain in the apartment. His family of course wanted him to stay put, but they suggested that if he had to move out, "Wouldn't it be nice if the two of them moved into a nursing home together?"

That proposal was rejected. The children knew their mother wanted to live in the apartment and that neither her mother nor they wanted to fund a nursing home for him. Instead, the widow's children insisted that he find a place for himself. His children asked her children to have him subsidize his new place "since she has money and he does not." Her children rejected that proposal as well, and shortly after he moved the widow and he quit seeing each other. The woman "took up" with one of her neighbors, an elderly gentleman who had his own apartment, and no drinking problem.

This story touches on many issues you and your children may encounter if you decide to take a partner in old age. Often, widows or widowers will have a boyfriend or girlfriend, fiancée or fiancé, or new spouse who occupy their residence, a living arrangement that can be a benefit or a burden—and sometimes both. Children's emotions are likely to run high when a parent remarries or starts a serious relationship late in life. Those emotions are compounded when that parent moves in with his or her partner. If you have children and you've never discussed the topic of companionship with them, they might not know how to treat such a relationship. Without understanding your priorities, the prospect of a new partner can be confusing for your children.

The media is full of stories about "gold-diggers," opportunists who target lonely, rich widows or widowers. These marriages generally result in arguments and fights over money with the widow or widower's children. Not as newsworthy, but perhaps more prevalent, is a parent's loving new partner and the family's gratitude for the emotional support and happiness of their parent. Frankly in my career, I have seen more of the latter, even if the new partner's motivation, at least in part, is a better financial future. However, most partners, whether young or old, are neither argumentative gold-diggers nor beloved new additions to the family. The children and advisors often have mixed feelings about them.

Many new partners who provide companionship and support may earn the gratitude and love of the children. Even at times where the motivation seems to be purely financial, the relationship may still work. Wise children recognize when a new partner is occupying the parent and relieving them of burdens. There are also children who resent any new partner of their parent; those battles are often the most difficult. As an aging wealth holder, you need to decide how to approach these relationships, preferably even before you enter into one, and how to candidly discuss them with your children and advisors.

BEING CLEAR ABOUT YOUR INTENTIONS

Late-life relationships can work well as long as there is clarity about your expectations and the burdens you are willing to bear. Will you be comfortable supporting a partner, taking him or her on trips, paying for dinners out, and generally allowing him or her to live off your wealth? Should your children or trustees try to protect your finances? Or should they assume you are happy to pay for the pleasure of a new partner's company? You need to discuss the issues and expectations likely to arise between your children and your partner's children as well. And you may also need to discuss your new relationship's impact on your prior marriage or an earlier relationship. These conversations should preferably take place before you have met a new partner, or when you are just taking up with one. Once you've had them, you'll be more comfortable in any new relationship you may enter into, enjoying the benefits of a compatible new partner.

Lawyers and family will generally recommend a pre-nuptial agreement for any subsequent marriage, and these are useful tools to start conversations about expectations with a prospective spouse. They allow clinical analysis of assets and set limitations on what may be required under various laws relating to divorce and forced shares of estates on death. But any negotiation of that agreement should be seen only as the start of the discussions that need to take place. They do not keep either spouse from doing more tham legally required and they do not represent the true and deep feelings of the parties.

For instance, a widow survived her husband, a fiery entrepreneur who had created huge wealth for himself, his wife, and their family. He died relatively young, and the widow remarried a well-established, divorced civic leader. They had a thoroughly drafted pre-nuptial agreement that set out all rights and responsibilities. Though he, too, was wealthy, unlike her first husband, he had inherited his fortune. Also, unlike her first husband—who believed her place was in the home, raising children—her second expected her to engage with him in the community. Together, they served on civic boards, developed deep friendships with other couples, and traveled often.

Over the twenty-five years they spent together, they led what most people would call a charmed life. They were pragmatic as well: They were always sensitive in keeping track of their assets. Each had children, and their children generally had good relationships with both of them. They were clear with their children early on that their wealth was to be kept separate, their expenditures fairly shared. Each had his or her own advisors, legal, financial, and otherwise. They explained they wanted to stay together, continuing to support each other well into old age, whether in good or ill health. They talked about their situations and preferences with their children and also exhibited their loving care for each over the years.

The couple lived into their nineties together, and their relationship stayed strong. When her husband started to suffer dementia, she was by his side. Even as he became less competent, there was no question about their loyalty to each other. However, if they had not been clear about their intentions, and if both had been less than competent, it might not have been apparent to their children. Their obligations to each other were mutual—he would have done the same for her and vice versa. Their children understood those wishes and respected them. Significantly, neither of them nor their children ever pulled out that pre-nuptial agreement. None of their conversations or legal documents referred to that agreement, and it was clear that over their marriage they completely forgot its terms.

Without any reference to that agreement, this couple took the time to ensure their mutual support was understood and accepted by their families. Communication with each other, their families, and their advisors was clear and direct. By talking with them about their plans and exhibiting the love they had for one another, there was no question about what should be done if either of them became ill.

MAKING YOUR PLANS KNOWN TO OTHERS

A husband whose wife was suffering from progressive dementia was physically and mentally exhausted by caring for her. When he could no longer handle it, and his own physician advised him that his wife needed more support than he could possibly provide, he arranged for her to live in a nursing home. The facility was equipped to care for those with her condition, and he was assured she would be attended to properly. Even though she no longer recognized him, he still visited her every week.

Their two children felt he should have maintained his caregiving role and kept their mother at home. Although they understood how hard it had been for him, and they knew about the advice he had received from his physician, they somewhat resented him for not sticking with his wife "in sickness and in health." He explained that he and his wife had always agreed that if either of them ever became fully incapacitated, the other should feel free to arrange affairs so he or she could live fully and independently. As he was finalizing his wife's move to the facility, his children listened to his words, but they were not completely convinced by them.

Shortly after his wife moved, he found a companion, a widow his age who had been friends with his wife. They spent time together and eventually she moved into his apartment, "sleeping in mother's bed," as one of the children described it to me. His children felt hurt and angry. They began to intrude on the relationship, questioning his decisions and his new partner's intentions. He knew they disapproved, but try as he might, he could not convince them that their mother would have approved. He said he and his wife had also agreed that under such circumstances, if the active partner wanted to seek companionship elsewhere, that was totally fine—encouraged even. In the case of the wife's dementia, she did not remember her husband, or children for that matter. The husband stuck to the plan.

By reaching such an agreement before either was incompetent, this man and his wife had made a reasonable, sound decision. However, their failure to communicate that decision caused unhappiness and distrust within the family. The man's children never felt comfortable with his new relationship, causing him to forever have a twinge of guilt whenever he was with them (though not when he was away from them). The discord affected their relationship for the rest of his life.

Wise spouses discuss their approach to future relationships in the event of death or incapacitation. Wise parents communicate those discussions and agreements to their children. Some couples reach agreement that a survivor should not remarry or should stay unmarried for a certain period of time. Of course, the wise husband and wife will recognize that the first to die or become incapacitated cannot legally prohibit the survivor from remarrying or from forming new relationships. Wills and trusts can be used to *limit* such developments, but even the tightest trust will not easily prevent a new relationship. And if that is the agreement, you must ask yourselves whether it is wise to share it with the rest of the family, as it may turn them into "enforcers" and affect family relationships.

It must start with a conversation between the spouses to ensure that they are comfortable with each other's intentions. These questions may help:

- When are new relationships appropriate to pursue— either before or after the death of your spouse?
- When is it appropriate to put you or your partner in a facility outside the house?
- How much of your joint wealth can be used to support a new partner, and what are your obligations to the children?
- How deep should a new relationship get?

Decisions designed to allow the survivor to have freedom to reengage at any time must be communicated while both spouses are alive and capable. Then, ideally, communication should continue after the death of the first spouse to ensure that wishes are respected. For example, a woman I knew took care of her ailing husband for many years. Early in their marriage, they had agreed that after the death of one, the other should feel free to remarry. "I always assumed he would, though he had no firm thoughts about my own plans," she told me.

After ten years of illness, her husband died. She called her daughters and told them she had had enough of taking care of a sick husband. She told them she had plenty of money (indeed she was quite wealthy) and that she never wanted to remarry. She started a life of travel and community engagement. No longer tethered to her house and caring for her husband, she frequently went abroad, both on her own and with friends. When she was home, she engaged in charity events and community activities. She served as a hostess at charitable balls with philanthropic donors, and partied night after night. She was extraordinarily active well into her nineties. She once said to me, "I am having the time of my life. I don't need full-time companionship and the obligation to consider someone else when I make plans. My life is perfect!"

Then she got very sick. The last two years of her life were spent in and out of hospitals with twenty-four-hour care at home. Her daughters were attentive, but it was hard for them as their mother developed dementia and was not entirely rational. A fifty-year-old male nurse was one of her caregivers and began to make unscheduled visits to see her. The daughters found this strange, but nothing could have prepared them for what came next. One day he told them, "Your mother and I are in love and we plan to marry." Her daughters knew she would refuse to remarry if she were thinking rationally—even if her suitor was a handsome man forty years her junior. Their mother had been crystal clear about her preferences early on, and that clarity allowed her children and trustees to take care of her. Without hesitation, the daughters engaged her attorney and together they ended the relationship with the fifty-year-old nurse. He disappeared and shortly after he married another man.

Another success story involved a widower of three months who remarried. His wife of thirty years had struggled with a terminal illness during her last year of life. A compassionate individual, the husband completely cared for her every need. After she died, he married a younger woman. The marriage seemed ideal to those of his friends who knew all three—the widower, his deceased wife, and his new wife. I asked his daughter how she felt about the remarriage. She said, "What a tribute that is to my mother and father. They obviously had great security in their relationship. They both told me that the survivor should always feel free to remarry. It reflected the pleasure embodied in their marriage. I am happy for all three of them." That outcome was the result of perfect preparation.

MANAGING NEW RELATIONSHIPS

A partner in old age can provide companionship. That individual can be someone to dine with, a plus-one at social engagements, a fellow traveler, a new "roommate," and a trusted counterpart offering various kinds of support. But when approaching new relationships, it's critical to discuss the type of support you're willing to give, as well as the limits of that support.

Consider this example. A widow in her eighties had a partner in his late seventies. The relationship was fairly new, but they had been enjoying each other's company and decided to travel together. They planned a two-week trip to London to stay at his favorite hotel. At her children's urging, the widow convinced her partner that they both get a physical before the trip to make sure no health issues came up while they were abroad. Her doctor told her she was in perfect health. Her partner's internist also met with her and said the same about him. "He is in perfect shape. He is not at any risk of any major—or even minor—health issues." They were both delighted, as were her children.

Off they went. Within a week of their arrival, he was rushed to the hospital unconscious. His liver had shut down, and he was deathly ill. The British doctors asked whether that had been a chronic condition. The widow replied she didn't think so. She called his two adult children in California. They told her the liver problem was actually chronic and had caused problems over the years. They were truly sorry to hear he was so ill and said they were so fortunate she was there to take care of him. They also explained they were both much too busy to go to London. "But do please call us every few days to let us know how dad is doing."

He was hospitalized for two weeks and spent another week recovering in their hotel room. The widow cared for him as best she could, but it was awful. She had few opportunities to go out and enjoy the city or even the amenities of the hotel. When they finally returned home, she called his internist and asked why he had not mentioned her partner's liver condition. His internist said, "Well, I knew he was quite sick and expected something like this would happen. But I did not want to deprive him of the fun of travel, and I did not want to worry you. So, I said he was fine."

That doctor apparently had no concern for the widow, effectively leaving her to care for her partner. If she knew she could have ended up in that situation, she would have preferred to stay home. "I cared for my husband through his long illness and had resolved not to remarry because I did not want to care for another husband," she explained. "I wanted to enjoy my old age. I liked this fellow, but I would never have agreed to have him as a patient!" She ended the relationship.

In the pursuit of a fulfilling life, individuals need to carefully evaluate the benefits and drawbacks of a new partner in old age. As with the widow mentioned above, the traumatizing experience of caring for a loved one in their final days may not be something to revisit, and understandably so. Though it may seem selfish to some, that woman did not sign up to be a "caretaker" for her new companion or a surrogate in the absence of his children. If the man had told her about his true health conditions—and if they had visited a physician that was loyal, objective, and reliable—she would have never gone on the trip. And maybe if she had known of his ill health, she would have at least spoken to his children about their availability to step in. Or possibly, she would have reconsidered their relationship all together—in your eighties, there's no point in wasting your time.

With this story in mind, ask yourself the following:

- How deep a relationship would be tolerable for you? Would you be willing to care for a new partner and their health complications once you're in your seventies? How about in your eighties or nineties?
- How much responsibility do you want to take on as a partner in a late-life relationship?

- If you were in such a position, would you have left your new partner in London and insist his children come take care of him?
- Or would you want to support your partner's illness, even paying for hospital fees and travel expenses?

It is not clear that the widow knew answers to any of these questions, other than she would not have willingly signed up for the responsibility if her partner's internist had been truthful. In reality, the partner knew he might get sick and that his children were unlikely to fly to England to care for him. He likely felt reassured that the widow would be willing take care of him, but it's obvious they never had such a discussion. It seems he was looking for support that he may have not been receiving from his family. Sad though that may be, it did not entitle him to create the situation he created in London.

A new partner may create demands for physical and mental support. He or she may also end up creating a need for financial support. Partners can be a wonderful resource to stave off loneliness in old age and help you continue to live a life full of love, joy, and excitement—but they can also be expensive. They may end up sharing a residence with you, along with care-givers, travel, and entertainment. So long as you are competent, you will be capable of deciding whether to handle those costs and how generous you want to be.

But as you become less competent, your children may need to decide what to pay for—and what not to pay for. They may even have to remove you from your decision-making authority as your cognitive abilities decline. What to them may seem a "waste of money" may to you seem appropriate for a terrific companion. This is why you need to discuss your priorities with your family and support team while you are still in the right state of mind. Whether your children or others, those taking care of you need to understand your expectations about the relationship and economics of any future partner. They may need to evaluate your financial situation to decide whether extravagant expenditures even make sense. They also need to understand your wishes to ensure future partners do not take advantage of you more than you would be willing if you were competent.

AVOIDING FINANCIAL EXPLOITATION

There are indeed financial opportunities to someone who enters into a romantic relationship with an elderly individual of means. Most of the time, this is not a concern, especially if the two people involved both have their own wealth or support from family. Unfortunately, there are the occasional situations in which one person in the relationship takes advantage of the other's wealth. This reminds me of a woman who made something of a career out of marrying old, well-to-do men. She carefully selected every husband to ensure that each was richer than the last, and she made a point of avoiding particularly healthy, younger men. Each of her husbands predeceased her.

One husband was my client, a widower, who was believed to be the richest man in his small, midwestern community. He loved her dearly throughout their four-year marriage, and despite an ironclad prenuptial agreement, he gave her more and more gifts as he aged. When he died, he left her most of his tangible property (household goods and the like) and a large part of his estate (much larger than was required under their pre-nuptial agreement). The widow had turned much of her husband's wealth into tangibles during their last year of marriage, knowing he would be leaving many of them to her. His art collection, for example, became extensive as she purchased artworks whenever she could. His children learned that his widow had also "invested" hundreds and thousands of dollars in household supplies, including a basement full of toilet papers and tissues.

Our client was this serial wife's third husband. The first husband had been the "love of her life" and had assets of relatively meager value. The second was allegedly a millionaire and died with a substantial, though not huge, estate. Our client was a high-net-worth individual and truly wealthy. He died with a $75 million-dollar estate (not counting the toilet paper and other tangibles.) After he died, his widow moved to a big city and married a man who was reputed to have hundreds of millions of dollars. Her love life was strategic and her fortune ever increasing, but she also apparently gave joy to more than her share of husbands. When she died several years ago, she was a very wealthy widow. She left her estate to her children by her first husband, the "love of her life."

If truth be told, our client and his widow's prior husband—whom I also knew—were both extraordinarily difficult people. Words like "penurious," "irascible," "heartless," "disagreeable," and "miserable" could have been easily applied to both of them. The wife was of strong character and seemed to thrive in relationships with these kinds of combative men. Our client's children were in their sixties at his death. They were well-taken care of by the gentleman's first wife, who had died during their marriage. Still, they ended up resenting their stepmother.

One of the children, a son who had never really worked, thought the widow had taken too much money. The other, his daughter, believed her stepmother may have overstepped her bounds. The daughter's husband, a wise and successful lawyer, had another point-of-view. He said, "She deserves every penny she gets. He was very hard work!" When all was said and done, their father died a happy man in that second marriage. "Gold-diggers" often have to endure hardship to earn their keep. It can be difficult for the family to feel grateful for the support and love they might provide, but maybe they should.

It should be observed that sometimes gold-diggers don't get the rewards they're chasing. Many years ago, an aging and very wealthy woman had diabetes when there was no cure for the disease. A rather disagreeable younger man "fell in love with her" and married her to the dismay of her parents, who couldn't stand him. To all appearances, he was simply waiting for her to die so he could inherit her estate. Her life expectancy was short, and he must have felt his reward would materialize quickly.

He made sure her estate was in order and always described her to his friends as "critically ill." He certainly would not have signed up for a long-term relationship—but then insulin was developed. For her, it was a "miracle cure." She lived another thirty years and survived her husband by five of those. As they were both Catholics, he had no way out of the marriage. She was saved by insulin; he was enslaved by it. His pot of gold never materialized.

There are also the rare instances in which a spouse kills a partner for money. A wealthy owner of a sports team on a weekend cruise with his wife is found washed up on shore after "falling off the boat." The wife inherits the sports team. Or a wealthy old woman is found shot and killed by intruders when her young husband returns from a business trip. He ends up with the house and all her assets. Needless to say, murder is best left to the imagination of Hollywood and suspense novelists—not wealth holders like you.

CONCLUSION

Whether or not you plan on relationships later in life, you need to be open about your intentions with your partners, your children, and your helping hands. You should be clear about what you want and don't want from late-life companionship. Partners can be a great source of enjoyment as you age, but they can also be a burden if you're not careful. Entering agreements (pre-nuptial and otherwise) can help start conversations and setting boundaries early on will help avoid those burdens and focus on the positives. You need to keep in mind how you will approach any new relationship and what that might mean in regard to your living situation, finances, and of course, your continued chase. You and your family should be wary of gold-diggers or others who may exploit you, but keep in mind that most people are simply looking for support and companionship to make their lives brighter and happier.

Chapter 7
Driving: Balancing Independence, Control, and Safety

The son of a 97-year-old woman called me one afternoon, urging me to tell his mother to quit driving. "Her eyesight is terrible!" he said. "She comes to my house for dinner once a week—a ten-mile trip each way—and I worry about her, not to mention everyone else on the road." I asked whether he had talked with his mother about his concerns.

"I couldn't possibly tell her to quit driving. She would be furious with me. But *you* might be able to convince her—or at least convince her to stop driving at night."

"Well," I said, "why not pick her up and return her home on those nights she comes to dinner?"

"Oh no," the son replied. "I don't want to waste my time driving over and taking her home again. Maybe you could tell her to take a cab or an Uber?"

"A cab?" I asked. "Your mother is worth hundreds of millions of dollars. Why not a nice car service or even a chauffeur?"

"I don't want her wasting money on that," said her son. "Better she should stay home or call a taxicab."

My conversation with his mother didn't go much better. When I spoke to her, she was intransigent: "I get great pleasure out of dinner with my son and his family, and whenever I drive, I stay off the highway and try not to go too fast. Besides, I often stop at the supermarket on the way, so I am already out anyhow."

Today, that woman is 100 years old and still driving! Fortunately, I do not live in her city (and I hope you don't either). I have, however, actually seen her behind the wheel since that conversation. I was with a colleague at the time who astutely observed, "That woman is driving like a bat out of hell."

There is almost no tougher issue for children than the question about an elderly parent's ability to drive. For many of those parents, driving is the ultimate symbol of independence and control. To them, giving it up means loss of both. "How dare my children take that away from me?" they ask. A parent who has taught a child how to drive at sixteen recoils at the notion of that very same child taking away that privilege as the parent ages. There's a practical concern here as well: For many aging wealth holders, driving is their main form of transportation, especially if they live somewhere without reliable bus or subway services. Without their cars, they could become fully immobile.

In the above story, the son should have developed a strategy to take his mother off the road earlier rather than later. By avoiding the issue altogether, he put her, and everyone in her path, in danger. (Except, maybe, himself: He refused to be a passenger when she drove or allow his children to be passengers in her car.) As discussed, the challenges of aging are often rooted in a tension between independence and safety. The two must be weighed against each other. Driving is a particularly complicated challenge because the safety of your passengers, other drivers, and pedestrians is just as much at risk as your own. Evaluating your driving capabilities requires a clear mind and an understanding of the grave risk to yourself and others. If you do not consider this balance of safety and independence while you are capable, you may reach a point in life where you can no longer appropriately assess the situation.

INDEPENDENCE VERSUS SAFETY

Sound analysis of this issue *cannot* start with the wealth holder saying, "I am willing to take the risks to maintain my independence." That position is not reasonable, since you'd be risking the safety of not just yourself, but others as well. The ninety-year-old man who thinks he put his car in reverse and instead drives headlong into a group of schoolchildren may survive, but he—and his family—have to live with the consequences. "Mother is willing to take the risks of driving" should never be a child's analysis either. Unfortunately, some children of aging wealth holders' take this position because it is the path of least resistance, or they believe the safety concerns are overblown. One client and friend once told me, "My father is ninety-eight years old and still driving. His eyesight is so poor he can barely tie his shoes, but he hops into his car and drives around town. Isn't that funny?"

"No, it isn't funny," I replied, "and *you* will be just as responsible if he hurts or kills someone."

Unfortunately, that was not the only time I've heard such a ridiculous statement. I often run into younger people who find humor in their parents continuing to drive when they clearly should not. It is not funny in the slightest, neither for the person driving nor for the public at large. (In 2020 alone, cars killed 42,060 people in the US; each year, as many Americans are killed in driving accidents as are killed by guns.[3]) But these sons and daughters don't seem to take into account the fact that they have an obligation to the surrounding community.

None of us wants to be the cause of such harm, no matter our age, but if you and your advisors (whether family or otherwise) don't plan when you're able, you will end up in an untenable situation. Considering the significance of these risks, when and how you should stop driving requires careful planning. If that planning does not take place when you're still a capable driver, your family and helping hands will have to take firm action later on regardless of your wishes. If they don't, the results could be dire.

It's easy to understand why so many aging individuals equate the loss of driving privileges with the loss of independence. In most communities, and for most people, driving translates into freedom, mobility, and even vitality. New York City may be easy without a car, but Los Angeles is not. My own great grandparents moved from a small town in southern Indiana to New York City, partly to be near one of their children, and partly to avoid the challenges of transportation in rural America.

For some, transportation options may not be easy to find if they want to maintain independence. Taxis may be available, and Uber or Lyft are smart alternatives. But during the Covid-19 pandemic, all of those options seemed less attractive because of the spread of such a highly contagious disease. It's true that the prospect of self-driving cars is not far off, and food delivery of all kinds is common. But none of these today replace the freedom to get into your car and go where you want, when you want.

It's useful to address these issues early on to avoid the type of problems a client of mine encountered as her husband's cognitive capability diminished. Driving was becoming more difficult for him. He had trouble braking, and he often lost track of where he was going. His doctor recommended he take a driving test and forbid him to drive until he passed with flying colors. He begrudgingly agreed.

Leaving the house the following morning, my client placed her husband's car keys in her upper drawer to help him avoid the temptation to drive. Within an hour, she received a call from him. "Where are my car keys?" he asked. She asked him why he wanted to know.

"Well," he said, "they are *my* keys after all; I should know where they are." Then he mentioned he might like to go to the club to meet some friends. She reminded him of the doctor's orders. "Well then, I won't go, but I need those keys in case there is an emergency." She asked what kind of emergency, and he said he might need something at the store. Finally, exhausted, she told him where to find the keys. Later she learned he had in fact driven to the club and got lost coming home. She was exasperated. To him, those keys and driving represented independence and safety. To her, those keys were a danger. How do you resolve such a conflict? The starting point is to separate mobility, and the independence it provides, from driving. "I want my car and I want to drive" is really a way of saying, "I want mobility."

TRANSPORTATION ALTERNATIVES

When we discuss driving and transportation, more often than not, what we're really talking about is *mobility*. As you age, you will want to stay mobile—it signals not just freedom but activity, strength, and capability. Still, you can remain mobile without driving. Plenty of twenty-two-year-olds living in New

York, London, Hong Kong, and other cities never drive at all, yet they get around just fine. Unless your dream is to become a long-distance hauler or a race car driver, you never truly need to sit behind the wheel of a car.

Fortunately, wealth offers alternatives unavailable to most people. A chauffeur is out of reach for all but a few Americans, but when private chauffeurs are an option, they provide both independence and privacy. With wealth, finding a caregiver with a chauffeur license may be an affordable alternative to driving. Limousines can also be scheduled for predictable journeys, though they are more difficult for spur of the moment errands. Of course, you can always pay someone to run those errands for you using delivery services, messengers, and the like.

Ultimately, it's clear most people don't want to quit driving. And like my client's husband looking for his keys, they come up with a multitude of reasons as to why—many of them questionable. A client and friend in her late eighties told me she hated taxis. "They are dirty and unreliable." She fought with caregivers who offered her rides as well. Though she had a smartphone, she never took the time to learn to use any of the apps, so Uber or Lyft was out of the question. And she wouldn't "be caught dead" on a bus. "I love to drive and always will," she told me one afternoon. She left my office and, shortly after, bought a new car, equipped with the most modern technology. Two weeks later, I saw her and asked her how it was coming along. "I am now homebound," she said. "I cannot figure out how to start it, how to take off the brake, or even how to adjust my mirrors." She became a prisoner in her own home, except when she cajoled her daughter into driving her around. In some ways, technology stole her independence, but if she had made alternate arrangements, she could have carried on with a full life.

My own father disposed of his car in his early seventies. He was a perfectly good driver, but it was one of the smartest, most rational decisions he ever made. Without a car, he started taking taxis to work every day, got rides to restaurants for lunch, attended social functions and get-togethers, and went any place he wanted to go with or without my mother (she drove for many more years; read on for the final outcome). I asked why he had given up driving when he was perfectly capable. "I want to start using taxis before I am forced to," he said. "I want to think of them as a luxury, not a replacement for something taken away from me against my wishes." He always enjoyed the conversations with the taxi drivers while maintaining a feeling of complete independence. In fact, once his doctor told him to quit smoking, he relished telling cab drivers who asked for permission to smoke while he was in their car. "I have no objection," he would say, "so long as we keep the windows closed."

Six elderly ladies I knew loved to go to the symphony on Saturdays. None was willing to be a passenger in the car of any of the others, particularly at night, and finding convenient, safe parking was a worry for all of them. Together they found a car service and reserved the driver for every Saturday evening. The driver picked up each one of them up at their homes and dropped them all off at the front door of symphony hall. The driver waited for them during the performance, and then drove each one of the women home after the concert, sometimes stopping for ice cream cones when requested. This arrangement gave all six women the needed mobility to attend an event and to feel carefree as they enjoyed the evening.

While you are still capable of analyzing your ability to drive, consider the alternatives. Many senior living facilities offer drivers. Some communities have services as part of their public transportation system where you can call for a ride, as compared to taking a bus or subway. And don't overlook apps like Uber and Lyft. It is certainly worth learning how to use them now, even if you don't intend to use them for years to come. No matter what alternatives you're considering, it all comes down to planning ahead.

MOBILITY PLANNING

Establishing a driving protocol will enable you to plan ahead for continued mobility. This approach means *you* retain control of any major related decision. Getting around as you would like is key to your independence, and your independence determines how you will continue chasing your dreams. So, what is good mobility planning? My father convinced himself he loved taxis. My great grandparents moved to Manhattan so they could walk everywhere. The ultra-wealthy can hire chauffeurs. As mentioned, everyone should have a smartphone and know how to use Uber or Lyft or, at the very least, have the number for a local taxi company at hand. Living near a child who drives might be helpful, too.

Any mobility planning needs criteria to guide when it's time to quit driving. When should an objective evaluation happen and who will be in charge of that process? Some states have laws that require a driving test at a certain age. Those laws remove the subjectivity about when it is time to get off the road. But for those who live in states without such laws, then what? At what point does someone ask your doctor to prescribe a driving test or insist you take one? These are hard questions to answer, but they should be considered while you're young enough to think about them rationally.

I had a thoughtful conversation with a sixty-five-year-old woman and her husband on this very topic. Both are quite healthy, and both drive without issue. Neither has lost any capability to think through the potential risks, and they were open to a comprehensive discussion of mobility planning. They agreed that so long either one was capable, that person would handle the driving. When neither was capable, they would hire a full-time chauffeur. The chauffeur could even be one of their caregivers. They also clearly stated that taxis, Uber, public transportation, and walking long distances were not their desired options.

Then I asked who would evaluate whether one or both were capable of driving safely. The option of periodic driving tests came up, and the couple felt such tests would be a good way to approach the decision. Who would ensure they were tested, and who would determine the intervals between driving tests? They agreed one of their children was quite reasonable, and she could be direct and firm. She was the logical choice to oversee this new "driving protocol." If she were not around, her brother would become the decision-maker. Then came the touchiest question of all.

"And at what age should the testing begin?" I asked.

"When I decide it is necessary," was the first answer. I explained that wouldn't work. They needed to come up with a concrete age and stick to it. The husband thought about it for a while, relented, and suggested age seventy-five. The wife agreed. She admitted they had a friend who had recently careened into a wall at age seventy-six.

The next day we met with the couple's two children. The mother explained that the daughter would be in charge of scheduling any necessary testing and analyzing the results.

Further, the mother said the son would take charge if the daughter could not. I noted that testing would begin at age seventy-five, and the daughter should arrange for each of them to be tested at that time. I looked to the mother for confirmation. "Well, yes seventy-five," she said, "but I can change my mind as I approach that age if I want to make it older."

"Yes, right, right," said the father. "We will let you know whether it is time for testing when we reach that age."

"That will not work," I said emphatically. As I made clear to the couple, such a plan was simply not feasible. Once you choose the age, it cannot be extended. In fact, there is no harm in sticking to the agreed-upon age. If seventy-five is too young, you will obviously pass the test; the only loss will be the time spent taking one. Thankfully, they concluded I was correct. The husband is now seventy-four, and I recently reminded him that he is a year away from the test. At least so far, he has not changed his mind.

DRIVER'S TESTS

You may live in one of the states that regularly requires tests for aging drivers. If so, consider yourself lucky. The decision is taken out of your, or your children's, or someone else's "helping" hands. If you don't live in one of these states, someone needs to ensure your driving skills are re-evaluated from time to time. If you pass the test, you can continue to drive. If you do not, it is time to stop. When that's the case, there needs to be a plan for mobility and transportation alternatives already in place so you can continue to get around as you would like.

My own mother was still driving at eighty-eight years old, and I worried about her. Missouri does not require a driver's test based on age, so I called the local DMV. I explained her age and asked whether they could retest her. They passed me on to their state agency in Jefferson City. What I was told was quite concerning: "Oh, Mr. Lowenhaupt, you don't want her retested. What if she failed? Then you would have to figure out how to get her around. We won't do that to you or to her."

I considered my options. One would be telling my mother "no more driving." In fact, my father did just that with his mother after she crashed into a brick wall. He made her give the car to her long-time housekeeper, who agreed to drive my grandmother wherever she wanted to go. He also cancelled my grandmother's insurance and had a policy issued in the housekeeper's name. Everyone was seemingly happy. Many years after the death of my grandmother and my father, the housekeeper told me with a smile, "Your grandmother never stopped driving. She would have me sit in the passenger seat as she drove 'her' car. She told me if her son ever asked, I should say I drove everywhere."

I feared a similar outcome with my mother. Trying to prohibit my mother's driving would probably not work and the conversation alone would likely sour our relationship. With some research, I discovered another option: a local hospital that gave driving tests based on a doctor's prescription. So, I called my mother's doctor the day before her annual physical and asked him to prescribe the test. I also told him to let my mother know it was *his* idea (and to keep my name out of it). At my mother's physical, he did both. She thought the idea of a test was humorous, but I took her to the hospital where the prescribed test was administered. She left in her car with the examiner, and I prepared for her to return with a failing grade.

Indeed, they both came back with smiles on their faces. "Your mother's driving is fine," said the examiner, "and she is one of the most charming students I have ever had."

I was surprised, to say the least, but I felt I had met my responsibility to protect others. At my urging, her doctor agreed to recommend the test every two years. Two years later, she left her annual physical with another prescription for a test. This time she had a different examiner, and when they returned, they had different expressions on their faces as well. He took me aside and said, "She stopped in the middle of the highway and then wanted to turn down the up ramp. She should never drive again." He repeated the same to my mother, saying her days behind the wheel had come to an end.

My mother was furious. She told me that the examiner was "rude and very irritable." She swore she was a capable driver and would take the test again. A week later, she actually took the written test but failed that one as well, followed by another test the next month. Thereafter, she used her younger house-keepers as drivers. And the streets of St. Louis have been safer ever since.

That she quit driving was fortunate. That she blamed the examiner and her internist, but not me, was fortunate as well. In fact, for several years after, she would tell me there was no reason she shouldn't be driving; I always nodded my head. We then agreed she would call her internist to ask him to prescribe the test again. He was somehow always too busy to write the script.

I have used the driving test prescription often with others, including an eighty-nine-year-old client who was actively driving his convertible wherever and whenever he wanted. A mutual friend called me one day, saying he was a menace. So, I called my client and suggested he ask his doctor to prescribe a driving test. He said that was entirely unnecessary, but out of respect for our relationship, he would.

Two weeks later, he called to report that his doctor had prescribed the test and he had taken it. The testing agent told him he was an excellent driver in all respects. "Do you want to see the report?" he asked, egging me on a bit. I told him I did, and he sent it. "The subject's driving is exceptional in all respects and would be for a man fifteen years younger. I endorse his continuing to drive." He drove that sportscar right up to the day before he died at age ninety-three.

CONCLUSION

Driving is one of the most difficult challenges to confront in old age. For most of us, driving represents mobility, freedom, and ultimately, independence. But these—and the related risks inherent in driving later in life—need to be weighed against safety, and not just your own, but also that of the people around you. Mobility, rather than driving, is what will actually help you maintain your independence and preserve your ability to go places when and as you want. Decide early how you will determine when you should quit driving. Set a date for testing if your jurisdiction does not require one and then stick to that date. Consider alternative forms of transportation to maintain your mobility—whether chauffeurs, taxis, Uber or Lyft, or public options. The chase requires mobility, not necessarily a seat behind the wheel.

CHAPTER 8
TRAVEL: CONTINUING THE JOURNEY AND NAVIGATING THE RISKS

A couple I knew often traveled around the world for extended periods. They had the wealth to maintain multiple vacation homes in Europe and a yacht capable of navigating the world. They loved the adventure of seeing new places and meeting new people, and they had the means to travel in luxury. In time, those extended trips got longer and longer: six months on the French Riviera, a few in Bali, a month back in the U.S. at their favorite ski resort, then off to the boat, letting the winds take them where they pleased. It may have been a little extravagant, but it was a terrific life, and they recognized how fortunate they were to continue living it for so many years.

But as they aged, life got in the way of travel. At age eighty, the husband fell ill. The doctors said he would require long-term medical treatment at their local hospital once every two weeks. Neither he nor his wife wanted to give up their lifestyle, so together they chartered an alternate course. Rather than regretting their loss of freedom, they worked with their doctor and the hospital. They developed a plan that allowed him to receive regular treatment, but still maintain some freedom to travel: They would come home every two weeks for that one day. They always managed to be close enough to an airport so they could arrange a private plane to pick them up and fly them home. There, they were met at the airport by a driver who dropped him off at the hospital and took her to their apartment, where she reviewed mail and ensured everything was in order. Then they were off again the next morning. They continued to travel as much as they wanted up until their deaths.

These two were lucky. After all, he only needed treatment every two weeks. But in another way, luck had nothing to do with it. They took the time to talk over their options and make plans so they could continue chasing their dreams. Not everyone has that luck and the wealth to plan as that couple planned. After many years of travel—whether to the other side of the world, the other side of town, or the other side of the room—freedom can come to an abrupt halt. Many forces can slow or halt your travel as you age: pandemics can result in legal limitations, personal medical issues can keep you near your medical providers, and travel risks can multiply to limit mobility. In effect, old age can become a tether, keeping you homebound, dreaming of all the past vacations you were fortunate enough to experience in your youth.

For many of us, maintaining the ability to travel—whether to pursue business, see the world, cruise the sea, visit museums and sites near and far, or spend time with grandchildren—is central to our vision for old age. If your travel is somehow limited, or if the travel door seems to close, it can feel like imprisonment. However, with planning and the acceptance of some potential risks, travel can be managed, and your wanderlust can continue. With forward thinking, your wealth can ensure safety, comfort, and excitement.

Continuing to Travel

Wise travelers plan their strategies while they still can. For example, if you like cruises, that may include regularly using the same ship or cruise line. Instead of adding an extra leg to your journey and flying to a different locale, you can sign up for cruises boarding in your own home country. You and your travel companions can also arrange an escort to the boat and prearrange for special needs with the cruise line. My own grandparents continued to travel as they aged. When they were younger, they often took small freighter ships, their loose itineraries full of spontaneity. Though they loved the adventure, there was one caveat: There were no doctors on these boats. As they got older, they recognized the potential need for medical attention so, they found larger freighters, big enough to require doctors. With this strategy they continued the pleasure of going places on simple boats with surprise stops and no particular itinerary. Yet, they were safe and comfortable.

For the aging traveler, flying may present challenges, but there are a growing number of services to manage those inconveniences. Airlines are often willing to meet you and escort you during departure, layovers, and arrivals. They usually charge a fee for this accommodation, but it is well worth it. Indeed, I once challenged a global airline to meet me on arrival in Sydney and have my checked suitcase in hand, so I didn't need to wait at the baggage carousel. They did just that! They ushered me through immigration and out a door to my waiting driver. I found I could do that in city after city, and it certainly made travel easier.

In addition to upgrading your accommodations, you can also plan around major family or social events and necessary procedures, appointments, and medical treatments (like the couple in the story at the start of this chapter). I've seen this strategy work time and again. "My doctor told me we could arrange my cancer treatments, so that my travel will not be impacted," one client told me. "After all, what good is my health if I am too busy trying to nurture it to enjoy the world?" He arranged his two years of cancer treatment to ensure he had periods of international travel—and his treatment was successful.

Another smart planner was an elderly gentleman who loved visiting London. He spent many a leisurely hour there, studying in the libraries, walking along the Thames, and finding interesting restaurants with hearty food and tasty ale. He had always been very active. As walking became painful in his later years, he faced the prospect of staying home. Instead, he found an apartment in London with an elevator, located near the library (and a good pub). He then engaged an excellent housekeeping service whose staff member served as a companion and hailed taxis for him. He also found a college student to help him in the library. With such full support, he managed to visit London year after year well into his nineties.

No matter what approach you take to increase the comfort and enjoyment of travel, remember it all comes down to deliberate planning. That's the approach favored by a San Francisco couple I know who spend six months a year in Paris and London. They started doing so in their early seventies. Renting apartments in each city, they built daily routines of walking through the surrounding neighborhoods and enjoying all they had to offer, whether museums or restaurants or libraries. They stopped at cafes to chat with locals and ex-pats, went to nearby concerts, and generally took in all of the rich history and culture of both cities. As they aged, they strategically got to know the city services in each location to help them get around town. They found a reliable driver in each city as well, and restaurants in the neighborhoods of their preferred apartments. Their forward planning will allow them to continue spending six months a year in London and Paris, independence intact, for years to come.

Planning ahead is necessary, but it doesn't have to be viewed as a chore. It can actually be fun. Finding your destination, studying and selecting hotels or accommodations, discovering what museums to visit and when, and booking restaurants reservations and sightseeing tours are all exciting pre-travel planning. Consulting with expert travel agents and travel services can also help. As you age, though, preparation needs to take into account more than just the best sights and restaurants. Your doctor may clear you for travel, but you should always know where and how to get to a hospital. Of course, there are scores of places—both urban and rural—that have easy access to competent healthcare facilities. By understanding and planning for potential risks, you will all but guarantee an excellent experience, no matter where you roam.

RISKS OF TRAVEL

As noted earlier, travel risks increase as you age. You are far from home doctors. Children and other family are remote. You must pay more for comfort and safety. Generally, travel is more arduous. Thus, it is important to recognize risks, balance them against rewards, and take steps to mitigate them. Luckily, wealth can help minimize those risks and ease travel, making the options for travel and accommodations nearly endless. But you must account for all contingencies and plan accordingly.

HEALTH AND SAFETY

An eighty-year-old client and his younger wife decided to take a cruise together in Alaska. This gentleman had a heart condition, but neither of them seemed all that concerned about it. They took some precautions, making upgrades to their travel plans so he could be more comfortable and ensuring there was a medical staff on board. They planned ahead, said bon voyage to their families, and off they went. Ten days into the trip, he died suddenly on the ship. The captain buried him at sea, and his wife continued the cruise. When she came home, she was grieving, but she was pleased they had that last vacation. She said, "We had discussed the risks we were taking and understood them. But we agreed they were worth taking to have the trip we had always wanted."

The world is full of elderly traveler warriors with medical conditions. They do just fine. Medications can be taken, doctors can be visited, and as discussed, treatments can be administered if scheduled appropriately. Still, there are many individuals—young and old—who run into health scares and medical emergencies while travelling. If they are abroad, the risks may be elevated due to lower-quality or inaccessible care.

For example, during the summer of 1964, when I was still a high school student, I lived in Japan. A group of us were taken to climb Mt. Fuji with an American chaperone in his early thirties. After we had the ceremonial "slide" down the volcanic gravel from Mt. Fuji, our chaperone had an appendicitis attack at the base of the mountain. There in a local hospital, without anesthetic, his appendix was removed. After a few nights rest he returned to the tour.

The experience today in Japan would be completely different since the country is replete with modern medical facilities. But recently a sixty-year-old I knew in perfect health took her two teenage sons to Bhutan to hike in the mountains. High in the Himalayas, she developed a serious medical issue. She was taken by mule to a local hospital, where medical personnel diagnosed her illness and performed a somewhat primitive operation. Her sons called her husband, and the three of them panicked. At midnight, the husband contacted a member of the family's support team, the head of their family office. From afar, the office took on the responsibility of arranging the woman's medical procedure and getting her home.

Planning every detail and arranging every necessary step in the process, this family office executive hired a jet to take the patient from the Paro airport in Bhutan to New Delhi. After she was rushed through the city's chaotic airport, she and her family were placed on a commercial flight that brought them back to the U.S. As soon as that woman recovered, she resumed her traveling. She has visited many parts of the world throughout her life since—always prepared for danger.

Another friend of mine, a woman with an intrepid sense of adventure, continued her travels late into life. At age eighty, she wired home that she had tripped on a sidewalk in rural Japan and fallen on her elbow, breaking her arm and badly bruising herself. Her children wired back: "Come home now." She sent a telegram in reply: "Having too much fun. Stop." And she carried on. In weighing the risks of travelling with a broken arm against the pleasure of travelling Japan, pleasure won out.

Similarly, a ninety-two-year-old client asked her daughter

to take her on a cruise in Alaska. They chose a ship with a doctor and small infirmary. They took other precautions as necessary and planned ahead, weighing the challenges and risks. Together, they concluded the trip was as safe as it could be. While on board, the mother decided they should sign up for the helicopter excursion, in which they would land on an iceberg. The trip was uneventful until their helicopter hit an air pocket on the return to the ship and bounced hard enough to break the mother's hip. She was taken to the ship and then to a hospital (again by helicopter) where her hip was pinned. "It was a wonderful cruise," the mother said later on, "and well worth a broken hip."

The risk of illness or injury while abroad can be covered by various forms of insurance, but many of them are not available to people over a certain age. Still, it's worth looking into what may be available and getting the advice of an insurance professional. And if insurance is not available, don't give up so easily: If you still want to travel, study the costs of adequate medical care where you want to go. High-quality medical care is increasingly available in many parts of the world. In some places, it's actually much less expensive than in the U.S. There are now travel physicians in the US who can even be retained for twenty-four-hour telephone consultation and advice.

Another novel approach gaining popularity is travel as an alternative to a nursing home. That, too, has risks and requires careful planning, but it can work quite well. I knew a ninety-five-year-old who essentially used cruises as places where she could be taken care of much more pleasantly than in a nursing home. She spent nine or ten months a year under the expert care of staff and crew, always on the same luxury lines. Staff escorted her from her cabin to the dining room, to the deck, or anywhere else she wanted to go on the ship, and she was always the center of attention. Her children flew to various ports to meet her and enjoy time together. The luxury cruise lines welcomed her as a special guest.

Until recently, this plan was relatively unique—quite brave and strategic. In fact, more and more people are using cruise lines for these purposes. With the Covid-19 pandemic, this approach may be more challenging and less desirable, due to the same concerns people now have over the safety of nursing homes. During the height of the pandemic, many cruise ships became hotbeds for the virus. As Covid becomes a routine and treatable medical condition, cruise ships may re-emerge as support centers, but in the meantime, the pandemic will continue to present risks to travelers' health and safety.

PANDEMIC CONCERNS

Though no one knows what will happen in the months and years to come, it is certain that the pandemic has affected our lives in unforeseen ways. This includes the emergence of new health and travel-related safety risks. Travelers during the pandemic have to consider potential exposure on planes, in hotels, at restaurants, or any other public place they go. The world is full of folks who tested positive for Covid on a trip and were forced to quarantine in remote locations until their home country deemed it safe for them to return. And then there were border closings. Any number of people found themselves locked down in various countries, unable to return to the U.S. and vice versa.

Even before tests and protocols were in place, I was scheduled to travel to Brazil on March 2, 2020, just a week or two before the U.S. went into full lockdown. Brazil had no reported cases, but as my travel date approached, I consulted Brazilian experts in security and health to ask if they thought the virus might be circulating undetected in the country. They believed it was possible, but at the time, there were few indications that the virus would become as deadly and widespread as it eventually did. I remained resolute; I was going on the trip. That was until March 1, when the U.S. government closed certain country's borders to returning citizens. Although Brazil was not one of them, I cancelled my trip out of concern I could be shut out of the U.S. Many elderly travelers had a similar experience. Being older and marooned in a foreign country can pose almost insurmountable challenges. The inaccessibility to family, home amenities, and first-rate medical care can be frightening.

Going forward, new protocols and safety concerns will likely affect how, when, and where we travel. Pre-trip testing, isolation when the disease is contracted, and other inconveniences have become common. Friends returning to Hong Kong—where, as of this writing, the Chinese are currently imposing their "zero tolerance" policy—were met at the airport by police. They were then locked in a hotel room for two weeks, their food delivered daily to their door. No fresh air, exercise, or even housekeeping or room service for them! Other countries—such as Australia and Singapore—have put similar policies in place.

Before the pandemic, globetrotting was so easy for people with wealth that many almost took it for granted. Maybe you were one of them. One friend living in Arizona explained at the time, "Travel is second nature to me. I can go to New York for an evening of theater. I can go to Paris for dinner. And I can go to Hong Kong to see my tailor. I don't worry about distance."

That friend may have been more casual than most. But before Covid, wealthy individuals and families were resourcing travel agents online, flying on jets (commercial or private) to exotic locales, booking cruises to every destination possible, and staying in international hotels. Paying for anything with credit cards and getting local cash through ubiquitous ATMs made travel infinitely easier than 100 years ago. If you were one of these lucky individuals, indeed, the world was your oyster.

Whereas in February of 2020 you could go to Paris for dinner or Hong Kong for a tailor, in May of the same year you could not walk down the street to dine in a local restaurant. Paul Fussell, in his book *Abroad*, gave us a historical comparison. During the years between World War I and World War II, the British created some of the greatest travel books. With the end of World War I, they were free to leave the island and travel abroad. But World War II dropped the curtain on that creative period. The British were again limited to their own island, their wings clipped. The pandemic left all of us stranded on an island as World War II left England.

Even as people return to travel, the services they had come to expect from hotels, restaurants, and airlines may seem limited. As of early 2022, many destinations were still inaccessible or dangerous because of the pandemic. No matter how old you are, when you are homebound due to a pandemic, it is easy to appreciate how aging homebound travelers can feel. The pandemic made us all appreciate the freedom of travel more than ever.

I saw this dawn of realization hit a forty-year-old man caring for his parents in their seventies. He had been discouraging his parents from traveling. He considered their travel worrisome and wanted to keep them "safe and sound" at home.

In 2019, he told me, "I can't understand the appeal of traveling at their age—after all they don't walk as well as they once did, and they are no longer perfectly lucid." Meanwhile, he and his wife were going just about everywhere in the world—safaris in Africa, beaches in the Pacific, museums in European capitals. A year into the pandemic—after a year in which the son and his wife had spent day after day at home—the son admitted, "I now understand why my parents don't want to quit traveling. It is in our blood. It represents the freedom we all want in our lives. And I will encourage them to travel again when they and we can."

INCREASING COSTS

The costs of comfortable travel increase with age. For example, a summer visit to Nantucket may be have been a breeze when you were forty, but that visit has likely become much more complicated since you've gotten older. You will likely need to bring more luggage, plan further ahead, and pay a premium to avoid the aches and pains that can come with taxis, commercial flights, and public ferries. Two ninety-eight-year-olds I know continued going to the island every summer by chartering a private jet, getting them there safely and avoiding congested airports.

Another woman told me, "Of course we use private jets to go to our Michigan house in the summer. How else could we get there? My husband has a whole crate of medical devices we must travel with. We could never fly commercial."

These couples are not alone. There was increased use of private jets during the pandemic as older wealth holders ventured forth but wanted to avoid public airports and crowded planes. With a little bit of creativity, and a great deal of wealth, they were able to bypass these issues all together.

For many people, arranging a private jet is a smart solution to the usual challenges of flying commercially. In fact, the costs can seem bearable compared to the alternative of staying home. If available, take advantage of private transportation. That is the favored approach of a couple I know living in Hong Kong. They regularly brought their grandchildren to the U.S. for family vacations to cities and places of interest. The couple was wealthy enough to own private jets (two of them), but neither jet could fly across the Pacific. Instead, they arranged first-class seats for themselves from Hong Kong to Los Angeles with business class seats for the children, grandchildren, and nannies (often on flights separate from theirs). On arrival in Los Angeles, the couple was met by one of their private jets and flown to the next destination. They arranged for the rest of the family entourage to be met by their other private jet in Los Angeles, then flown to meet them wherever they were going. Travel for them was stress free.

Another friend of mine from Hong Kong traveled extensively into her nineties—always first class. "My children ask me whether it is extravagant to always fly first class," she said to me one day. "I tell them that if *I* don't fly first class, then when I am dead, *they* will. I'd rather do it myself."

If you have a family office, the office can hire full time travel experts—health and transportation—to manage all of your and your family's travel. If you do not have a family office, you can engage the services of travel health "concierges," or "concierge doctors" (discussed in Chapter 4), who are available twenty-four hours a day to advise you on health emergencies while traveling. Some will even fly to you if necessary. You can also hire specialized travel agents who remain available twenty-four hours a day to help you deal with any flight or lodging issue abroad. Hiring such experts is not cheap, but the expense may well be worth the freedom and independence that come with a carefree journey.

COMMUNICATING WITH ADVISORS AND SUPPORT TEAM

As with any other planning for aging, it is crucial to communicate your plans and wishes while you are still sharp. If you have a family office, make sure they know exactly the risks you're willing to take while traveling. Likewise, make sure your spouse or partner and children understand them, too. Failure to communicate with your advisors and support team when you are young can ground you in old age when you're really looking to soar. Clear communication about the risks you're willing to incur is paramount to leading the life you desire.

An elderly man I knew ensured that his globe-trotting would continue by being crystal clear with his support team. The man split his time between the savannahs of Tanzania and his home in Connecticut, six months in each location. As he aged, he developed dementia, and in time, it worsened significantly. His children said, "He won't know where he is, let's put him in a nursing home in Hartford—he'll be happy there. All of that travel back and forth is becoming dangerous with his condition." His wife refused. She explained that long before his illness, he had told her that the regular travel between the two continents was what he wanted most, no matter the risks, inconvenience, or expense. His wife intended to honor that wish, and she continued to regularly take him back and forth to Africa.

If you haven't made your wishes clear, you should. Otherwise, your children or trustees may conclude that your travel is an extravagance and should not be encouraged or facilitated. For example, critical medical equipment needed by an aging parent is often seen by family as problematic and expensive. One client whose mother had dementia explained it this way: "She wants to visit her sister in Italy. That's fine until you consider that she would need a companion the entire time—and I am too busy." She went on to point out that her mother's brain was "too addled to recognize that the whole idea is impractical. The airplanes would be very difficult with wheelchairs and the like. And the costs are really not justified. She would never want to incur them." I knew that mother well. She would have been more than happy to incur the costs, and more than willing to hire a companion. But her children made those decisions for her. They concluded that "mother would *not* want to travel if she could understand the challenges and costs."

Frankly, in this case, I could not tell whether the children's concern was entirely for their mother. Perhaps it was more about their own convenience and a desire to save their eventual inheritance. Why were they unwilling to travel with her or hire a travel companion to allow her to see her sister? The situation would have been different if the mother had planned ahead by making sure her support team understood her wishes.

CONCLUSION

Travel, whether to see the world, to see family, or to conduct business can be lifelong. Age and health may impose some limitations but with some forethought and strategizing, you can mitigate the health, wellness, and safety issues while main-taining mobility. Figure out how to secure adequate healthcare while traveling, taking advantage of potential insurance options or the use of concierge doctors. Consider private jets. Choose locations with at least decent medical care. And ensure that your team of advisors knows what you want if a difficult situation arises. Engage your family in conversation and explain why taking measured risks, paying for a traveling companion, and spending on first-class travel are all worth it. With proper planning, the intrepid traveler does not need to be imprisoned by old age.

CHAPTER 9
LEGACY: ENHANCING AND PROTECTING YOUR REPUTATION

A man I once knew built a large business with a number of shareholders and a capable board of directors. A major shareholder himself, he spent considerable effort devising a qualified board and succession plan. As he aged and became less capable, his board effectively fired him as CEO and removed him from the board. He was outraged and miserable. "How dare they?" he said to his wife and children over and over. Stewing over the situation, he often seemed angry and annoyed. In reality, his business had fired him at the right time, actively ensuring its ongoing operations while preserving his reputation as a captain of industry. The board's action would protect both of them; he didn't see it that way, however.

He channeled his disappointment, anger, and extra free time into a local charity where, for years, he had previously served as the President of the Board of Trustees. With seniority, he had attained a role as an "Advisory Board Member," entitling him to invitations to all board meetings. His family considered his involvement in the charity a productive way for him to spend his time—an alternative to the business. They figured this would be the best option to "keep Dad occupied and away from the business, where he could have done real harm." At first, that charity board thought of his increasing incapacity as a kind of eccentricity. But within a year, his behavior became distracting and his participation in board meetings more difficult.

As the man descended into dementia, he left his wife and took up with a twenty-five-year-old woman (one-third his age). He moved into her apartment and paid her rent. His family was enraged, but he claimed he was "happy as a person can be." He started showing up at the charity board meetings with his new girlfriend, who drove him to each and every one, and he often monopolized board deliberations by talking endlessly without much logic. He even attended a meeting in which the two of them sat in a corner of the room holding hands, kissing, and whispering to each other.

As an "Advisory Board Member," he had an ex-officio seat on the charity board, and pursuant to its bylaws, the board could not remove him or fail to send him the required meeting notices. His family no longer considered his involvement "a good way to keep him busy" and felt terribly embarrassed by his behavior. Frankly, they wished he'd just disappear. Still, they had no control over the situation, other than to telephone the charity president and ask that he not invite him to any further meetings, an action the president could not take under the bylaws.

Ultimately, the man married his girlfriend, and his new wife promptly had him put into a nursing home without any ability to get out. Locked away, he could no longer attend the board meetings. His new wife's decision to commit him saved the charity the awkwardness of trying to keep him out. The new wife lived independently—and happily spent all her husband's money. His reputation was destroyed, and his significant business and community achievements were soon forgotten. The legacy he had created over many years was ruined.

As you've aged, thoughts about your legacy have likely become more prevalent. Maybe they've even taken center stage. Questions such as, "How will my legacy be built?" "Where will it be built?" "Will it be built at all?" All of these considerations probably run through your head regularly. Will you be remembered for your work, your art, your philanthropy, your family? Will you be remembered for the dreams you've chased and how you've chased them? Continuing your chase as you age can further enhance your legacy. At the very least, one of your goals in later life should be the preservation of that legacy.

Yet, old age can tragically destroy your reputation. Without forethought and planning, you may wind up regarded as nothing more than an old fool while you are alive, and long after you're gone. In fact, the world is *full* of old fools, people who have lost their dignity for one reason or another. Some had strong legacies at one time; others never had any legacy to destroy. The old fool is unlikely to be respected: "Poor guy—he has no family, no business . . . and no marbles," is not how you want people to speak about you. We would all rather hear: "How well he has aged—in control and so generous and thoughtful."

Dignity as you age helps support legacy, and such dignity comes from developing strategies to avoid becoming that old fool. Those strategies may be realized through helping younger people, planting the "trees" for future generations, engaging with your community, continuing employment, or simply taking a step back to enjoy your wealth and time among family and friends.

SERVING OTHERS

Serving others is usually the key to successfully building a business or a reputation. The great thinker, the diplomat, the successful political leader, or the intelligent counselor builds legacy on the basis of what he or she does for the community. For wealth creators, their vision directs their efforts. They ask, "What need am I fulfilling?" Apple Founder Steve Jobs probably said it best in articulating the future needs of customers: "Our job is to figure out what they're going to want before they do."

Visionaries in the U.S. and Europe helped globalize manufacturing and finance. Technology pioneers in Silicon Valley revolutionized every aspect of modern work and life. In the process, prolific wealth was created for the founders of Apple, Microsoft, Amazon, Tesla, Meta, and others. As important, these companies benefitted myriad stakeholders— surely a proud legacy for any wealth creator. In short, these visionaries have changed and improved their communities— and the entire world.

So, significant wealth creation happens when a product, service, or solution meets a genuine need, whether it is consumed locally or globally. As these founders and leaders create a business that fulfills that need, their reputation in that community—however that is defined—grows with its commercial success. Such visionaries usually end up with a strong legacy. They often preserve and burnish that legacy in old age with civic engagement as volunteers or philanthropists. Such civic leadership and community involvement follow because these individuals are viewed as capable and responsible leaders.

However, their success is really the result of their vision and efforts in earlier years. Success in serving others then becomes key to enhancing their legacies.

CIVIC LEADERSHIP AND COMMUNITY INVOLVEMENT

A client of mine was the head of a research team in the Manhattan Project. His success and experience led to an outstanding business career, ultimately as CEO of a major US corporation. Upon his retirement, he became a dedicated philanthropist and the Chairman of the Board of a major university. His reputation covered many fields: science, business, and education. Yet his motivation to build community was consistent throughout each field. Many people did not recognize this fact, until later in his life, his granddaughter wrote a book about him (discussed in Chapter 13), explaining his role in the Manhattan Project and his lifelong motivation to help others.

Indeed, many wealthy individuals who were not wealth *creators* per se—including wealth inheritors and professionals with substantial careers—build legacy by directly assisting their communities. For example, a physician I know who had retired from medicine spearheaded an extraordinary community development program in a lower-income neighborhood. After having cared for people through his medical practice for years, he worked to create affordable housing that was desperately needed. A mergers and acquisitions lawyer I know—as well paid as any in the country—retired from law and volunteered in a public defender's office to mentor students in providing legal services to the needy.

Though many wealth creators and wealth holders turn to philanthropy later in life, it's never too early to start this planning. Legacy is built over a lifetime and starting community involvement early helps as you get older. It also allows your children to watch and learn involvement. An elderly philanthropist and I once led a program for young entrepreneurs. The philanthropist claimed these students would, of course, be too young and busy to "worry" about philanthropy. He thought they should wait until, like him, they were old, their children grown, and their businesses sold. "Meanwhile," he said, "as a parent you are busy building your business, but you should tell your young children to volunteer and give money to charity." His idea to be directive with children but otherwise wait was wrong, and I told him so. Those young entrepreneurs needed to start planting the seeds of philanthropy as soon as possible for two main reasons.

First, individuals need engagement outside of their businesses, so the dream or vision they are chasing can continue even after leaving business. Otherwise, the exit from the business ends the chase, and they are left with nothing to work toward. They need to keep growing their legacies in other ways. The mission these individuals planned to pursue in old age should be as engaging as the mission of building their businesses. Second, and just as important, young children need to see the evolution of their parents' legacy, which can serve as a model for their own community engagement. Simply telling your children to volunteer—or to give a portion of their allowances to charity—is not enough. They need to see *you* actively engaged in your business and in your community. Simply put, volunteerism and civic engagement should not be roles only for young children and old people.

A friend of mine who built a successful investment business was strategically intentional about his legacy. His business was successful, in part, because he satisfied a previously unfulfilled niche in the investment world. In his fifties, he began collecting a specific genre of art. As the collection grew, he created a foundation to encourage museums to show his art to the public. He gave much of his collection to the foundation, so it could lend the art to museums and provide grants to study it. In his sixties, he called to tell me he was selling the business, and for a very high price, he noted.

When I asked him why, he explained, "My passion has become my art and my foundation. The world needs to see this collection and meeting that need is now my vision and passion. I want to devote myself to this full time and don't want the bother of the business. Someone else can run that and continue to meet my clients' investment needs." As planned, he sold his business and fully gave his attention, time, and effort to the foundation. After easily transitioning from one chase to another—from building a business to meet one need to introducing the world to another—that man will continue to build his legacy for many years to come.

AVOIDING A NEGATIVE LEGACY

There are also wealth creators that still serve others by continuing to run companies in industries they have for decades. It is not unusual to find perfectly competent ninety-year-olds—such as a Warren Buffet—overseeing their companies. If they continue to operate them well, they may indeed maintain their reputation for many years to come. However, keep in mind, legacy and reputation can become more positive or negative as you age. Enhancing, preserving, or improving both requires a well-defined strategy. Without a strategy, you may end up with a negative legacy that you will have to work hard to "fix."

In fact, history is full of wealth creators who have tried to rebrand their negative legacies. The Sackler family, whose name has become synonymous with the deadly opioid epidemic, sought to establish their legacy through community engagement, namely gifts to museums and universities. J. P. Morgan had the same goal in mind with his philanthropy. Michael Milken, former junk bond king and pardoned felon, attempted a similar feat with his philanthropy and the Milken Institute, now one of the country's premier leadership forums.

But such efforts don't always work. The Sacklers will likely be remembered for their role in the opioid crisis, not their many financial contributions to the art world. Though J. P. Morgan is thought of as a philanthropist by some, others consider him a robber baron of the highest degree. Milken's time in jail for financial shenanigans (securities and reporting violations), may overshadow the groups he has founded and the research he funded about melanoma and other deadly diseases. The point is that you must be as strategic in preserving your legacy as you are in building it.

THE OLD FOOL TRAP

Whether you serve others in the profit or not-for-profit world, you must plan ahead to avoid becoming the "old fool." Achieving that goal requires parallel strategies. You must first create a support structure to ensure you will be able to continue chasing your dream. Next, that structure must provide for objective oversight, protecting you from bad judgment in old age. This "governance structure" can come from protective trusts, well-designed professional guidance, or a clear understanding of your wishes.

Protocols and protections need to be in place to keep you on track or slow you down if you end up becoming derailed.

This is the reason a durable power of attorney, a revocable trust, and a sound business structure with strong succession plans become critical. (More on succession planning in Chapter 10.) Having these governing structures in place, and easily available, allows you to rely on others when you decide you want or need help. Most of all, these safeguards will help you maintain your dignity, and in doing so, preserve your legacy.

PROTECTIVE GOVERNANCE STRUCTURES

A fellow in his mid-sixties was considered the premier tax accountant in his community, representing some of its wealthiest and smartest residents. He worked alone, and his wife and children never fully understood his business. This accountant was extraordinarily intelligent and considered himself extraordinarily wise. He'd spent years building his legacy, and it was to be one of brilliance, attention to detail, and shrewdness in all respects.

Then in his late seventies, he was approached by a team selling an oil and gas tax shelter. They told him many of his clients may not understand the shelter, but considering his background, experience, and investment savvy, he would have no problem seeing its great value. They gave him volumes of records to review. Everything he read convinced him this shelter would save his clients millions of dollars in taxes. His due diligence was not complete until one of the salesmen on the team flew him to Venezuela, where he was shown "the oil wells being drilled and gushing with 'black gold.'" He felt this was an amazing opportunity, and he convinced his clients to invest with him in the venture.

In fact, he was so enthusiastic that he invested most of his own substantial net worth as well. He was convinced he would be as wealthy as his wealthiest clients by the time he retired. What he failed to recognize was that a mere ten years earlier, he would have advised against any such plan—it was too good to be true. Still, as the reported value of the venture soared, he enjoyed "'incredible' tax savings on account of the drilling." He gained further tax deductions by making substantial charitable gifts, with buildings and endowments being named in his honor. Proud of his accomplishments throughout life, this would be his crowning achievement.

That's when the Securities and Exchange Commission (SEC) decided to look into the venture. The SEC found that the whole scheme was a massive fraud. That sales team owned nothing and produced nothing, other than profits for the promoters. The venture became known as the largest investment fraud of the era. Notes were found in the firm's files targeting this specific accountant. One memo even stated, "A fool but he might be smart enough to figure this out if we give him too much." The oil wells he had seen gushing belonged to Standard Oil of New Jersey, but the profiteers had removed any signs indicating ownership before they flew him down.

The accountant's clients who had invested with him in this fund all concluded he was either an old fool or a crook. He was the former, but that didn't matter to those people who believed he was the latter. The charities he had so generously funded threatened to remove his name from the buildings and endowments unless he replenished the investments, which were now worthless. His family was also without his investments. He had to continue to work until his death without the savings he had planned to use in retirement. In the final insult to injury, the IRS asserted substantial tax deficiencies (in the millions), not only for the worthless charitable gifts, but also because none of the drilling and exploration had actually taken place. He spent years arguing with the IRS and finally lost. And he lived the rest of his life known as an old fool.

How could he have avoided being duped and ruining his reputation? He should have created a structure for his business to provide support as he aged. A business partner might have slowed him down and discouraged him from selling the fund to clients. Maybe the partner would have applied different rules and seen through the ruse. Alternatively, a good lawyer or another accountant might have dissuaded him from going "whole hog" on this investment. Instead, all he had was a simple revocable trust, of which he was sole trustee! He had no guard, protections, or support from falling into the old fool trap.

To avoid such a fate, put a strong governance structure in place. This can take a number of forms. Similar to having helping hands support you, strong governance and the corresponding legal instruments can help manage what you do not want to, or can no longer, manage. They will also protect you as your capabilities start to diminish. A close family member or reliable professional advisor can be particularly helpful if you already rely on them. Indeed, a loyal secretary or assistant can often keep track of your business, mental or physical health, and executive function, and make sure there are no dangers on the horizon.

Revocable trusts, as outlined in Chapter 2, can be a fine resource depending on the trustees you've selected. As discussed, selecting those trustees carefully and strategically is of paramount importance. The aging accountant should not have been the only trustee of his revocable trust. A co-trustee should have been involved to ensure his decisions were sound and to recognize an apparent decline in his mental acuity.

Co-trustees could have continued to help the accountant without forcing him to be declared "incompetent" by a doctor or, worse, a court. Such trustee provisions work well. They often allow for a seamless transition from a competent creator to a team that can help preserve the individual's dignity and legacy.

Unfortunately, the story of the foolish accountant and his tax shelter happens too often. Lack of planning can create financial hardship for the old fool and his or her family, but it also threatens one's legacy. Sometimes even when a plan is in place, it might not be sufficient. The plan needs to ensure that the right people have the right powers when the time comes.

REMEMBER TO PICK THE RIGHT TRUSTEES

One respected civic leader I knew had all the necessary trustee provisions in his revocable trust, but it turned out he had the wrong trustees. The document provided that when he was incapacitated, his three children would take over his role. Throughout his career, that civic leader had been a trustee for a number of people, and he had served on any number of boards, both corporate and civic. He understood the concepts of trusteeship and the challenges of selecting effective trustees. But when it came to his own family, he let sentiment get in the way and was blind to his poor decision. Two of his children were close, but they did not get along with his third. They considered the third profligate, and they resented gifts their father gave him.

This civic leader had been ably served by an accountant who had been in the family business for years. By then, he was running the father's small family office. As the father got older and dementia began to set in, with the help of his accountant, he was coping well enough—or so it seemed. Yet, the two children who were close together believed it was time to wrest power from their father. They found a doctor to declare him incompetent. Meanwhile, the third child hired another doctor to declare the father *competent*. A court battle ensued.

The two children painted their father as an old fool—a womanizer unable to discern right from wrong and completely without any financial capability. The suit hit local newspapers, and the father became distraught. He could not understand the details, and he kept asking his accountant to straighten everything out. The accountant was powerless. The three children ultimately settled, but only after their father's reputation was shattered and his dignity lost.

If that father had named professional, objective co-trustees, they could have managed his affairs. The independent co-trustees would have crafted a plan to support the supposedly "profligate" son, if that was what he needed, while allowing the father to remain a trustee with his full dignity intact. Sadly, that civic leader did not create a governance plan that worked. He lived for over 100 years, but at his death, he was remembered as much for the family battle and his foolishness as for his accomplishments.

COMMUNITY ENGAGEMENT RISKS

Even if the proper governance structures are in place, maintaining community engagement as you age can still be difficult. Volunteer work, board service, charitable giving, other forms of philanthropy—all can be satisfying. But they can also be time-consuming and increasingly complicated as your capabilities wane. As noted, civic engagement can be a wonderful way to spend your later years, but there are risks that are rarely addressed. (Consider the business leader in our opening story.) Indeed, a charitable endeavor is one way families put old fools out to pasture, but the old fool's incompetency can be a distraction—or worse—for the charity.

If you've ever been involved on a charity board, you've likely heard statements similar to the following:

- "Poor Mary. She cannot remember anything, so we ignore her in board meetings. Not sure what to do about it."
- "John had a stroke and is having difficulty getting to meetings. His wife says his judgment can't be relied on, and he probably shouldn't be on the board. But how do we ask him to leave without hurting his feelings?"
- "Bill's drinking problem has gotten the better of him. Should we move our meetings to the morning, so he doesn't have so much time to drink before we gather? As Chairman, his condition in the afternoon makes it hard to get anything accomplished."

Forgetfulness, illness, addiction—any or all can affect one's ability to function later in life. If you plan to engage in the community, you need to recognize these possibilities and put the appropriate guardrails in place. Not only is this the right thing to do for the people with whom you are working, but it will also help you keep your legacy intact.

One captain of industry I knew retired with great wealth. He had houses in his hometown, Phoenix, and Cape Cod. Throughout his career, he had held civic roles in a number of organizations, but he decided that in retirement, he wanted to help educate children. He joined a tutoring program that worked with disadvantaged kids after school. All went well for several years, but then his capabilities, judgment, mental state, and executive function all started to deteriorate. At home, his wife noticed he frequently became confused and unable to control his temper. He would fly into fits of rage over trivial matters, but she attributed that to his frustration. "He needs to keep busy," she said. "Otherwise, he becomes frustrated and then angry." She encouraged him to spend more time tutoring.

Neither she nor those involved in the tutoring program realized he was exhibiting that same anger and rage with the children. Finally, one of the children disclosed that the man had become furious with her only because she misspelled a word, even threatening to hit her. After the child's parents told the tutoring agency, it came to light that other children had been having similar experiences with him. The agency terminated the relationship. At his urging, his family unwisely tried to take the agency to task for "rejecting" the valuable services of this well-respected "captain" of industry. The publicity resulted in his disgrace, and the community branded him as unstable and potentially dangerous. He and his wife moved to Phoenix full time, and he left behind a reputation that was much worse than just that of an "old fool."

When I talked to his wife and children, they admitted they had noticed strange behavior as he aged. But they couldn't imagine that his behavior took place outside of the house. "We thought it was good for him to get out and tutor those children. After all, he was giving them an unparalleled experience considering all of his knowledge and accomplishments," said his wife. She continued, "He would be so ashamed if we tried to get psychiatric help or had spoken to anyone about ending his volunteer work." How sad that he and his family had not considered and planned for his mental decline. They all failed in their responsibility to protect those children from his anger and instability.

Just as there are a number of opportunities for reputational damage in volunteer work, there are risks in board service as well. Old fools insist on remaining on boards or in leadership roles in various groups, even when they should know better. How often do you hear of people resigning from civic boards for "health reasons?" The answer is probably, "Not often enough." A case in point is the gentleman from the story that began this chapter, who let his legacy fall apart.

CONTINGENCIES FOR YOUR OWN CHARITY

The key considerations for establishing a governance structure may be even more complex if you are planning your own foundation or charity. Ask yourself, is that structure going to be a "safety net" for your incapacity? And what level of independence will you enjoy? If you set it up as a family foundation, you may decide that other family members will ensure it continues under your leadership and with your dignity intact, even if you are no longer truly at the helm. If you create an independent board, it will have its own perceptions of reputation and fiduciary responsibilities, which it may exercise less sensitively to your wishes.

A founder and executive director of an active youth program came to me and said he wanted to assemble such an independent board. He was getting old and believed a good board would perpetuate the program after his death. His plan was to populate the board with well-qualified experts in the field. I reminded him that an independent board could fire him, but he wasn't worried. He simply assumed the board would recognize that because of his background and expertise, they could never replace him. I pressed him to reconsider, but he wouldn't hear of it. He created an independent board of experts and gave it full authority to run the program.

Within a year, that board fired him. A young PhD in educational theory was hired to lead the organization. The board praised the founder and wished him well on his way out, but they had been eager since day one to exercise their prerogative to get rid of him. They formally let donors and alumni of the program know that the founder had been ousted. They informally told anyone who asked that he was "well past his prime" and that their decision had been made for the good of the organization. Though the program prospered, its founder was forever after unhappy.

Another family I knew set up a charity to continue the work of their mother. As we formed the charity, I asked whether the family wanted a "family charity" or an "independent charity." Initially, the family thought they wanted everything to be independent, even though the members recognized that all funding would come from the family. Indeed, other family members felt they would like roles in the charity operation as well. After several discussions, it was decided the charity should be a "family charity," and the board should be solely made up of family members. The family became invested in the charity, financially and emotionally. It was indeed part of the mother's "legacy" and remained so. But it also became part of the family legacy. Family members performed well beyond mere "fiduciary duty" to honor their mother and enhance her reputation. That successful charity is now twenty-five years old and continues full steam ahead in its second generation of family leadership.

Another charity founder insisted she wanted an independent board that would employ herself, her husband, and two of her children. She planned to avoid any challenge to her leadership role on the board by appointing only friends who "admired" her. Although she was indeed admirable, with a long legacy of success managing the charity, as she aged, she became less and less competent. Her husband became less energetic. And her children seemed to be drawing their salaries without doing any work. She did not notice how the operation was faltering, and her husband and children seemed not to care. Rather than trying to fix the situation—by retiring the founder and firing her husband and children—the board members began to resign. She simply found other admirers to replace them.

Meanwhile, a friend from outside the charity found a possible "merger" partner. The board members all thought that was a great solution to the problem and brought it to the founder's attention. She reacted angrily. The partner was not up to her "standards," and she would not hear of the transaction. Rather than insisting on the transaction, a majority of the board resigned; the rest passively let her have her way. These "friends" were all torn between their loyalty and admiration for the founder and their duty to do what was right. For ten years, board members came and went while the charity spiraled downward. Without a strong governing board or a family that was fully invested in the success of the charity, the charity failed entirely. The founder was devastated.

One of the most interesting examples of a business legacy that went sideways is the reputation of Bill Gates. Indeed, in the early 2000s, Gates was known for Microsoft and the great wealth he had built from it (then maybe anti-trust violations).

Over the years, Gates's father worked with him and his former wife, Melinda, to build a prominent foundation. In 2020, the name "Gates" was associated with public health and education initiatives in Africa through the Bill and Melinda Gates Foundation.

Bill Gates's father has since died. Bill and Melinda Gates have divorced. Controversy has swirled. In ten years, will the mention of Bill Gates conjure a torrid divorce and accusations of employee dalliances and sexual improprieties? Where were the governance structures, the family support needed to keep Gates on track, preserving the legacy he and his father had built together? Will he be remembered as an old fool? His challenge is now to build a "safety net" to help protect his legacy.

Conclusion

Your reputation can evolve without much attention to it, but it is crucial to think of it strategically, particularly as you age. While you are relatively young, you need to consider how your reputation is developing and what your legacy will look like. Ask yourself, "What do I represent to my children, my community, and my colleagues?" You may well find you need further work to create the ideal or to preserve what you have. Whether and how you will be remembered, therefore, requires careful planning. The strategy needs to be built around the dream you are chasing and the support you will need to help you continue that chase, without becoming an "old fool." Creating your legacy or redirecting it well can take a lifetime, but it can be obliterated in a split-second, whether by illness, incompetence, or the loss of executive function. Before you allow your legacy to be shattered, plan ahead and prepare now.

Chapter 10
Relevance: Continuing to Provide Value as You Age

A third-generation family business was run by three brothers. Two of them headed their own divisions in the company. The third, a lawyer, was a board member. All three of them had children, but the two brothers who actively led divisions died relatively young. Their children, some of whom were just infants, weren't ready to take over the operations. Managing the business fell to the remaining brother, the lawyer, who did not have the business acumen to run those enterprises as he freely admitted. He had never planned on taking over the company, and his brothers had never planned on passing away at such a young age. In fact, none of them had prepared for these untimely deaths. So, the lawyer brother hired professional managers as the fourth generation matured. And he began developing a plan to allow for the next generation ultimately to take over the business.

When one of the children was old enough to enter the business after a spell outside the company, the surviving brother brought him into the company and placed him in a management position. He encouraged the company's CEO to train the young man and provide him with guidance. That young man grew into a senior management role and accepted greater responsibilities. The surviving brother eventually had all of the family's fourth-generation members join the governing board, while he remained chairman.

He strategically transformed the chairmanship into a position that enabled the fourth generation to truly govern while helping the board implement generous retirement programs for the company's professional managers. He deliberately helped the fourth generation design a management structure involving all of them but placed one of them clearly in charge. In time, that surviving brother gradually ceded governance responsibility to the group. Within thirty years of the deaths of the two managing brothers, the family business had prospered and was being actively run and governed by the children of all three brothers.

That effective succession plan came about not through ponderous governing documents, nor through family mission statements or constitutions. Rather, the result was a product of strategic planning by one wise elderly family member. On the death of his brothers, he could have simply taken over and tried to run the company even without the background or skill to do so. Alternatively, he could have stepped aside as he aged and let the business go as it might. Instead, the surviving brother enhanced his value to the family and company by ushering in a new generation with precision and care.

This plan involved many years of deliberation and focus, and it included conversations with the entire family. That planning was fundamentally about roles: the surviving brother defined a role for himself that changed throughout the transition and proved invaluable. There were also clearly defined roles for the existing professional managers and CEO, the new fourth-generation manager, and all of the family board members. The success of this plan was nearly unparalleled. Unfortunately, without a plan in place, succession is often a disaster. Few business owners have wise brothers who will ensure that the next generation can take over, or even that the business will survive.

For the business and the family, that story is a story about succession. It is told often by the wise brother and others in the family as an example of how to build succession management in a family business. As that it is not easily replicated since most families don't have the wise brother and the next generation ready to work together to succeed. The more replicable part of that story is what it meant to the wise brother. As he aged, he maintained his value by defining role and strategy to benefit the business. In fact, the children, the in-laws, and the employees all considered him indispensable and respected, admired and loved him. He was self-actualized as he aged, and he had satisfaction that comes with success.

Maintaining your value to a business or organization as you age can prove difficult if you allow yourself to stagnate. Too often, without having thought ahead, older business managers or owners will simply decide to keep doing what they've been doing for ages, whether it makes sense to or not. You need to find a role that suits you, your abilities, and frankly, your short-comings, if you plan to stay active in a business or leadership role. And as the brother in the preceding story proves, that role may change over time.

No matter what situation you design for yourself, you want it to be one in which you can provide value, whether as an advisor, a mentor, or a board member. You'll also need to recognize when you can no longer provide that value, and then design a graceful exit. In some cases, your consistent presence may be the link that holds a business—or even a family—together. This kind of planning may take more effort and coordination, depending on the structure of the organization and what part you have played historically. Nowhere is the challenge more complicated than in the "family business."

THE "FAMILY BUSINESS"

If you run a family business, you need to address an important question while you are still young enough to do so: What is the relationship of the business and your family members? Answers may include:

- To create wealth, stability, and comfort for your family
- To give your children, whether all or one, a business that will be theirs to run, including any related work and roles you have held in the community
- To allow you to build and operate the business any way you choose and let your family have what is left at your death

There's no wrong answer, but you do need to be intentional about defining that relationship. If you want to pass the business down, as many family business owners do, a comprehensive succession plan must be in place. Part of your value will come from designing and implementing that plan.

Such a plan will contain a long list of questions. But before you design the plan you must start planning by recognizing whether or not you truly have, or desire, a "family business" and how that relates to your "family wealth." Until the family members' roles within the business are clear and the strategies are well defined, your business is likely to experience dysfunction.

This process requires you to consider what truly makes a business a *family* business. The world is full of commercial entities called "family businesses" founded by successful wealth creators. Yet, few of those founders have ever stopped to ask: What makes their businesses "family" businesses in the first place? For instance, a businessman I knew created a successful company. He liked to talk about "family business" and "family wealth" with his four children, then in their forties. Three of the children had mid-level jobs at the company, and the fourth knew she could always go to work there. The father ran everything, and the children were tirelessly vying for his attention, each hoping to be named his successor. The board of the business consisted of the father, the mother, and the family lawyer, though the father regularly called "family meetings" where he sat at the head of a table and talked about the business and his successes.

Family dinners turned into "business dinners," at which the father and children "discussed" the business, and their spouses rather competitively traded success stories about their own children. Competition among the four children became extreme. I even attended a family dinner at which the four started fighting, the mother burst into tears, and two of the children left the dinner with spouses trailing before dessert could be served.

As the situation became unbearable, the father and mother came to me for advice to restore family harmony. I asked the two in a private meeting: "You call this a 'family business' and you talk about 'family wealth.' What is it you really mean by those words?" The father launched into a long exposition about the importance of family—a value instilled by his own parents—and how he was passing that value down to his children. He was taking them to "family wealth" conferences so they could understand what they would be inheriting, how much they were receiving, and how important their role would be some day.

"Yes," I said, "that's all fine and good, but what makes this a 'family business?' It is really your business and your wealth. When you die, what is left can be for the family."

There was a brief pause, a moment of silence as the husband and wife exchanged glances. Then the husband replied, "Of course," he said. "No one ever described it that way." He had attended conference after conference and studied all sorts of books, but he had never articulated this fundamental fact: This business was entirely his.

We then had a family meeting at which the father told his children that, unequivocally, the business actually belonged to him, not "to the family." They all needed to understand that they would have no rights in the business before he died. Having led them to mistakenly believe this was "their business," he now realized he had done a disservice to himself and his children. He explained that he could, and would, decide what to do with the business on his own terms. When he died, whatever was left—whether the business, wealth, or both—would belong to his wife and children.

He ended that meeting by pronouncing, "The rule will be that I make the rules . . . and I alone can change the rules." He also explained they should not consider the rules as set in stone. In fact, they should not rely on what may be a rule one day because it could change the next. We ultimately softened that pronouncement by saying that when he articulated a "commitment," rather than a "rule," he could not change it. For example, he created a rule that he would help purchase houses for his children, but that could change depending on the circumstances. But he committed to pay for private schools for his grandchildren, no matter what.

The children now had clarity and understood that, despite their quibbling and positioning for control, their dad would run everything involved in the business. Though not without some resentment at first, they were able to get on with their lives once that was spelled out. It ended the family meetings and created harmony among the children. Never before had they felt like a team together, fully living with the facts of the business control. Their father ran that business into his nineties. He also ran it into the ground. It was his to lose, and he did.

Luckily, his wife had the foresight to squirrel away a substantial amount of wealth outside the business. Meanwhile, each of the children led productive lives outside of the business, earning their own money and following their own dreams. Without their father's clarity, they would have never taken that step. They would have likely still been waiting for their father's "final decision." Though it may have seemed harsh and irrational at the time, his value was actually his honesty and openness. And though it often works out otherwise, by maintaining a consistent role, he indirectly provided value to his family, even if his business suffered in the end. Unfortunately, that's not always the case.

"SOME DAY THIS WILL ALL BE YOURS (MAYBE)"

If you are part of a true family business, you must decide how you will continue adding value as you age. What role will keep you engaged and constructive? If you have decided you want to keep the business "in the family," your value will be in planning for the future with your trusted advisors and the family members who will be involved. Strategies will be necessary to reach your goals and to allow your children enough time to build their own lives. Though it should be obvious, many family patriarchs and matriarchs seem to forget that as they age, so do their children. You will not succeed in old age unless you start thinking about these matters when you are young enough to think clearly.

More often than not, roles are never made clear in "family businesses." Nor are expectations or plans for the future. Children may believe their parents are making promises to them without ever confirming that is truly the case. Or founders may look at their children as the ultimate successors, even when those children are much too young to know whether they will be interested or qualified for the positions. Such assumptions sow confusion, typically followed by conflict.

Willingly or unwillingly, qualified or not, "next generation" executives may enter the family business regardless. Whether or not they are deemed competent by the founder is another story. In reality, maybe the next generation family members simply aren't interested. Maybe they don't have the passion or knack for the job. Maybe the dream they want to chase is much different than the one their parents did and cannot be realized within the family business.

Still, as a founder of a family business, you can continue adding value by having an open mind. Ask whether "family business" means that the "next gen" should be encouraged and given a leadership role no matter what. Few founders are wise in this regard. Instead, they often decide that the business should be sold because they believe the next gen is not as competent as they are. That decision—and a lucrative sale price—further validate the founder's business acumen objectively in terms of dollars and cents. If you take such an approach, that's fine, too. But it will require a redefinition of "family business" to mean that the value (and ensuing family wealth) belongs to the family, *not* the management of the business itself. And that redefinition needs to be conveyed clearly to the family.

Even though that sale can cause happiness among family members not involved in the business as they find themselves "rich," it can also create heartache for those who had hoped to build their careers in the family business. They may have expected gainful employment in a respected family business, a prominent role in the community, and a proud association— not money management. Often with the urging of the parent, the child "starts over," purchasing or creating a new business with crumbs from the sale of the old one. Undercapitalized and without any tolerance for risk, the new business fails within a few years. The "heir apparent" ends up middle aged and without any occupation besides stewarding "family wealth."

Another frequent scenario is the aging patriarch who will not give up the reins. That aging patriarch can add value running the business but will not add any value in terms of long-term perspective. My favorite example of this scenario was an experience I had as a young lawyer. My father and I were visiting two brothers who owned and ran a large foundry company. One brother was ninety and the other ninety-two. The seventy-year-old son of the ninety-year-old had worked in the business for forty years. My father asked the ninety-two-year-old, "How is your nephew doing?"

"Give him a few years more," said the uncle, "and he will be a pretty good foundryman." The brother nodded approvingly. In fact, that seventy-year-old predeceased his ninety-two-year-old uncle. He never had the next "few years" necessary to become "pretty good." Roles were never carefully considered because the brothers did not recognize the potential vulnerabilities that advancing age and death posed to the business. That business died with the last brother.

PLANNING FOR SUCCESSION

When it comes to a family business, a well-conceived succession plan is absolutely critical. Helping to create and implement that plan as you age can be much more valuable than simply continuing to run the business, as the opening story of this chapter illustrates. That plan requires carefully designed processes and deliberately assigned roles for everyone involved. It must be developed by answering questions of the highest importance, including:

- What is meant by "family business," and how can you articulate that so your advisors and family understand what is meant?
- What are the roles of various board members?
- Does the board act by consensus or simple majority?
- What are the rights of shareholders with respect to the board and the business operations?
- How are operations of different businesses delegated?
- How is the CEO selected?
- What are the expectations about family roles internally and externally as employees and as owners?

A key consideration is the expectations you have for *your* role as you age and the evolution of that role. What leadership can you exhibit to ensure the plan works? If there is enough clarity, the rest may be easy. Unfortunately, such clarity is not always easily expressed. Sometimes family succession works quite well, but success is usually the exception, not the rule. There can be no success unless there is some understanding of your role, and the limitations that may be imposed on you, as the patriarch or matriarch of a family business. And if your role is well defined and understood, you will maintain your value to the business.

As the leader or founder of a family business, you are likely concerned about the company's fortunes after you leave, especially if you are forced out. In Chapter 9, the wayward board member who created problems at his favorite charity due to his dementia turned out *not* to be a problem for his colleagues in his business. That's because there was a board governance structure that moved him out when it was time. A board can play an important role in succession management and the continued success of the business during and after a transition. But a board can also be a threat if you never plan to exit the business because you believe you will never need to be replaced. A board vote removing you from senior management and from the chairmanship of the board will be painful after you have devoted your career and wealth to it. The board will be evaluating your value objectively, and without a carefully delineated role that value will be low as you age.

I know one founder who was so worried about his possible removal from the board of his publicly held "family business" that he never formally served as a board member, even as he retained a substantial ownership interest. Instead, he arranged for the company's bylaws to provide for a lifetime appointment as an "advisory" board member entitled to attend all board meetings. "They can never remove me from that board," he said, "because I am not on it." A unique approach, but it worked well, at least for a time. The founder stayed fully involved as long as he could, and the board listened to his advice even though he had no official vote. As he began to lose his mental acuity, the board started to ignore his input entirely. After all, they had the right to do so and it was prudent governance to disregard him when he lost value.

TO RETIRE OR NOT TO RETIRE

A primary question that will come up time and again is when you will retire. As a business owner, you may have more options than most, but you also have more at stake—far more than an employee. The owner must demonstrate strategic value if the business is to prosper. Employees just need to do their job well. Whether you run a family business or not, if you have a valuable leadership position that you plan to leave some day, a thoughtful exit strategy must be designed and formalized many years in advance.

CREATING A STRATEGY

Any strong succession plan will address who decides when your exit is appropriate and how it will be accomplished. Exiting shareholders or owners are roles often covered explicitly in buyout agreements and other governance documents. How to transition management from one person to another is less often covered, and never nearly as well. In this respect, a graceful and effective exit strategy is almost always complicated, whether the governing board is made up of family or colleagues (or both). When it comes to family businesses, this is where process and clearly defined roles can tame unwieldy family dynamics. By creating a structure and plan ahead of time, you will protect the business and yourself.

But designing that plan is not easy. A plan that says, "I will resign when I decide it is time" rarely works. When a client of mine turned sixty, he announced he would retire at age seventy. All of his decisions were to be made based on that plan. For nine years, he repeated his intent; his board, employees, and family relied on it. When he was rounding the base to his seventieth birthday, his judgment and energy diminished, but they all said the business could survive the next year. His retirement would then resolve the problem of his declining capabilities. But on his sixty-ninth birthday he announced he had "changed" his mind. "I am hearty, capable, and doing such a good job running this business that I will postpone retirement until I am eighty." The business had no plan to move him along. Until his death, at seventy-eight, the business foundered.

If announcing your plans to retire in ten years won't work, what options are available? Often, trusted employees are put in a difficult corporate governance position when managing an owner's exit strategy. This is an especially important issue in a family business, where succession is challenging, and family dynamics are inevitable. Employees managing the process will age along with you, so when you are ninety, you will have lost some perspective. You'll think a sixty or seventy-year-old is quite young and maybe still not ready to take charge of your life's work (like the foundry brothers).

Even a more practical employee or younger advisor is likely to resist dislodging "the boss" no matter how poorly the owner is managing the business. Afterall, even if you are running your company into the ground, you're still the one writing the checks. Sometimes, a governing board can be made up of professional advisors, but they, too, can find it challenging to remove their clients. Trusted advisors—lawyers, accountants, or otherwise—may be willing to approach you, but as soon as you disagree with their assessment, they are in no position to argue.

As discussed in the previous chapter, you want to avoid becoming an old fool, but you might also feel in your heart of hearts that retirement isn't for you. Even if you announce a retirement date in advance, it's possible you'll change your mind. You may want to stay where the "action" is.

CHANGING YOUR ROLE FOR THE BETTER

If you are valuable to your business—or someone else's business—you can continue to play an important role for many years. If, on the other hand, you are unwilling to adapt to your age and condition, you will likely need to be eased out of the business altogether. There are many examples of principals and employees who remain valuable by evolving their roles as they age. As you contemplate stepping aside as CEO or from another leadership role, consider the following cases.

A friend of mine who is a nun ran a hospital well past any reasonable retirement age. Still, her order always supported her. When it was time for her to "slow down," she assumed a new position coordinating care for those in the order even older than she. Now in her late eighties, she is still responsible for the care of her older sisters. A loyal and effective employee can have an irreplaceable institutional memory well into his or her eighties. Age can even be a benefit by allowing employees to serve in roles that they couldn't manage (or imagine) when they were younger.

Another interesting example is the story of a Holocaust survivor I knew. He had been an attorney in Germany before World War II and immigrated to the US in his fifties and then went to work for a major corporation. Alas, the company made him retire at sixty-five, even though he was still wanted to work. He was unwilling to spend the rest of his life in retirement and instead got a part-time job at a manufacturing company. He worked for three brothers, owners, in their thirties who had also been Holocaust survivors. Recognizing his experience, the brothers quickly promoted him into a management role. Though he had no ownership, he was soon considered the "fourth," much older brother, equally running the company along with the other three.

As the three brothers aged, disagreements and arguments at occurred almost daily. However, the "eldest brother"—the attorney—always calmed the waters. He also began to effectively manage the firm's financial matters, working directly with accountants, the IRS, and others. Despite the familial infighting, the business prospered. Each brother attributed the success to the attorney's level-headedness, intelligence, and experience.

The attorney's service continued as he entered his nineties. And as he aged, the business became his life. He came to work every day, often staying ten hours, then he drove himself home at night. The brothers treated him with the utmost respect. They often went to his office for advice, and they made sure he had the best medical insurance available. After he was arrested for driving the wrong way on a highway off ramp, they set up a company account for him to use taxis to and from work.

The attorney was worth whatever the owners paid for health insurance and transportation. At age ninety-five, he brilliantly used his age for an important tax negotiation (and he remains the finest tax negotiator I have ever encountered). When the company was to undergo an audit, he was concerned about one issue that could be controversial and potentially result in the company owing millions of dollars. We discussed the issue and concluded there was a likely adverse assertion the IRS could make. I asked him whether he would like me to join him in the meetings with the IRS agent. He decided he would go it alone at the outset but call me in if he ran into any trouble.

After the meeting with the agent, he called me to say that the conversations went well and there had been no assertion of a tax deficiency. "I got along fine with the agent," he explained. The brothers and I were somewhat surprised, and we were unsure what arguments had prevailed—until I ran into the agent one day. The agent knew of my relationship with the company and volunteered that he had conducted the audit with the "old man."

"What a lovely old man he is" said the agent, "but he made it almost impossible for me to audit." I looked puzzled until the agent continued, "Don't you know he is deaf as deaf can be and he doesn't speak English? I couldn't start to explain any issue to him, and I couldn't possibly try to assert a tax deficiency on a complicated matter to a deaf man who can't speak English at ninety-five years old!" That old man cleverly used his advanced age as a negotiating tactic—a role he could never have played forty years earlier. He managed to mold his role to his age and his employer. The brothers valued him more than ever.

My grandfather's law partner, who was also my law partner and my father's law partner, was one of the greatest will and trust draftsmen of his generation. A brilliant mind, he dictated every will and trust to his secretary, sometimes keeping her at dictation for two or three days. He was also a professional magician and a personal friend of Houdini. His son joined the law firm when the partner was in his sixties and still quite active. But as our partner entered his mid-eighties, his capacity for detail started to wane. Soon after, his ability to walk diminished as well. His son drove him to work, and the two would walk together to lunch at a nearby diner every day at 11:30 am.

Over time, this valuable partner's clients had predeceased him, so he was no longer dictating those wills and trusts. Instead, he sat at his desk for eight hours a day, proofreading the wills and trusts written by other lawyers and reading legal journals. He was quick to correct any errors he found in the documents and often circulated articles he thought others should read. We were all happy to have his help.

With the caring support of his son and the value we placed on his advice and experience, this partner stayed "active" in the law firm until he passed away in his mid-nineties. He was always highly respected, and he found pleasure and pride in his daily activities. And even at that age, he would amaze visitors to the office, along with myself and our other lawyers, with his magic tricks and stories of Houdini. As he aged and lost some of the capacity that had made him a star, young lawyer, he managed to change his role to remain vital as a senior lawyer and font of wisdom. He stayed important, never losing his "magic" touch.

NOT CHANGING YOUR ROLE

The aforementioned stories show how some people can successfully "grow into" new roles as they age. But the business world is full of companies that have failed when their leadership has rigidly tried to perform the same roles for years and years (such as the patriarch of the family business discussed earlier in the chapter, who announced he made the rules and could change them). Not everyone can transition from a "sharp technical mind" to a "wise elder" without losing relevance and value.

Sadly, this was true of the Family Office Executive appointed by a wealth inheritor many years ago. The wealth inheritor established a family office and hired his accountant, then in his forties, to be the Family Office Executive. Twenty years later, when the inheritor died, the Family Office Executive continued working in the firm, now for the inheritor's children as they entered middle and old age.

When the last of the children died, the Family Office Executive was in his early nineties. He was a fixture in the office as the inheritor's grandchildren began to take over. The aging man saw his role as running the office and making sure the "girls and boys"—now in their sixties—did not spend too much money. He kept all the details of their wealth to himself and did not believe there should be transparency since, "if they know all they have, they will spend it all as well."

The older the Family Office Executive became, the more determined he was to keep "the boys and girls" from spending their money. Such a dynamic soon became untenable. The inheritors disliked his control, and anxiety was apparent at every family board meeting. Various board members found themselves feeling sick at the thought of attending these meetings, but they had little capability to express their anger. Fundamentally, they wanted to show respect for the old man, who went way back with the family, but their resentment grew by the day.

The old man lacked warmth and refused to play any role as mentor, which would have prepared the "children." Instead, he continued exerting the same amount of control as he did when the "girls and boys" were teenagers. Still, they gave him the benefit-of-the doubt, even as he tried to control their lives, with no sensitivity to their feelings as individuals. Their anger became redirected toward each other. Before long, there were numerous disagreements among the family members, who were now at various levels of estrangement from each other. They ultimately closed the family office—for their own sake—and gave the old man a generous (they would say "loving") retirement plan when he was ninety-four years old. They lived quite happily after that, and he lived long enough to remarry a younger woman who took care of him until his death at 103. Yet he never got over having been "let go."

Those children were torn between respect, loyalty, and care, as well as the obvious fact that the old man was too old and too controlling as he stepped into the shoes of their grandfather. He could no longer run the family office. They would have liked to support him—just as the old Holocaust survivor was supported or as our elderly partner at the law firm was supported. Yet, he really did not deserve that kind of support because he was unwilling to redefine his role. The result is that he ended up unhappy, forever feeling he was treated badly.

FINDING YOUR PERFECT ROLE

While you are young enough to objectively consider your future role in the business, imagine the role you'd like to play and the transition process. Share your decision with your support team, whether your board, your employer, your children, or your professional advisors. Discuss with them how they can facilitate the transition and how they can help evaluate when your ability to work is becoming limited. They need to know the plan *you* desire.

Certainly, the most effective way to proceed is to design your involvement to gradually diminish into a "lesser" role over time. The Holocaust survivor transitioned from being a day-to-day bookkeeper and manager of the company to a wise counselor. He continued to provide real value by helping the brothers make decisions and get along. He also used his age to benefit the business. Our law partner moved from dictating wills and trusts to reading others and scouring articles for relevant information.

They took on "age appropriate" roles and activities, and they were wise enough to do them by themselves (with a little support of course). As an aging lawyer myself, I always remind myself that good lawyers go through stages. Young lawyers have a keen intellect and are excellent at reading and interpreting statutes and regulations. They can sit in a library poring over books or can stare at a computer researching precedents and the like for hours. Middle-aged lawyers possess judgment and wisdom based on experience and can counsel clients facing difficult issues. Older lawyers have seniority and can speak with authority.

When I was a young lawyer, my father was a middle-aged lawyer on the verge of becoming an "old" lawyer. A new corporate client came to our firm with a state tax question, asking us to handle the case in Missouri. The client's counsel explained the arguments in the client's favor and let us get to work. As I drove my father home that night, he observed that the corporate counsel was missing an important argument, one relating to the state statute involved and the year of its adoption. "Until 1980 or so, that state tax law was based on the 1919 US Revenue act, and I expect that was true in many states." He sent me to the library. After hours of research, followed by memoranda, briefs, and arguments in court, my father's analysis won the court case, and the day, not only in Missouri but in other states as well. His brilliance saved the client tens of millions of dollars of taxes.

When our work was completed and the case won, my father sent the corporate client a bill for $75,000 "for miscellaneous services rendered," a relatively large bill for that time. The corporate counsel called my father and asked that the statement and bill reflect the hours spent, as required by his company. My father said, "That is easy sir. I decided not to bill for all the time we spent researching and writing memoranda and briefs. That was done by a young lawyer, and it was a very good experience for him. I didn't want to charge for his time." He continued, "Instead I charged only for my time. I bill at $300,000 dollars per hour and your case took me fifteen minutes to analyze and come up with the argument that won you tens of millions of dollars." There was a moment of silence before the corporate lawyer said, "Thank you" and hung up. We received a check for the full amount the following morning.

My father would not have spent the hours in the library doing the work I could do and should have done. His age and station in life would have made that difficult. But his value—at $300,000 per hour—was clear to everyone, and on that basis, he remained an active partner in the firm up until his death.

CONCLUSION

In planning for aging, consider the value you have provided for a business or organization and how it should change as you get older. If you want to stay active in a business you or your family own or in another business, consider what you can truly do well in old age, not just what you have always done in the past. Over time, your role will change, and that's a good thing. It ensures your well-being and the health of the organization. That role should always be considered in light of a "succession" plan for a family business. In many respects there are two separate issues: What is a good succession plan? And what role should you play in it? You can help answer both questions but ultimately your feeling of satisfaction in aging will be grounded in your playing a constructive role in that plan.

If you lead a family business, know that any succession plan can be complicated, but none more so than when planning in a family business. Roles are often unclear, exit strategies undefined. In any succession planning within a family business, you need to discuss your plans with the members of the family, so they know your wishes and expectations. You also have to create clearly defined roles. Whether you own a business or work for someone else's company, a strategy should always be in place to maintain value as long as you can. And when you cannot maintain value, ensure you have an exit strategy that will work for you and the organization.

CHAPTER 11

COLLECTIONS: BUILDING, ORGANIZING, AND LETTING GO

A client and friend had three major collections of books, artwork and ephemera, each among the greatest in the world. He had fallen into his obsession in college, but after a successful career and an early retirement, his collections grew dramatically. By his late seventies, one collection had over 15,000 items and was worth well over $50 million. He lent his objects to world-class museums, many of which built exhibitions around them and produced catalogs purchased by other museums (and studied by other collectors). To track these pieces, he spent many hours meticulously organizing his files, but he still kept many details in his head. Whenever he and I discussed his plans for the collections, his conclusion was, "First, let me get them perfect. They need completion and thorough cataloguing. Then I can consider what to do about them." Unfortunately, he never stated how the collections would be handled if he became incapacitated or "if" he died. Instead, he flirted with various museums and promised, someday, to make up his mind as to the disposition of his collections. Many museums were waiting, and hoping, to take them on.

This man was lucky in a number of ways. He chased pieces all over the world, and with plenty of money, he could purchase whatever item he wanted, regardless of price. He also had a wife who thought of this passion for collecting as part of his charm. She took a certain pride in it and tolerated the time and energy he spent on collecting and cataloguing, as well as the inordinate amount of space those collections occupied in their house. But his greatest good fortune was that he died suddenly, without any period in which he lost competence. Up until that moment, he had remained fulfilled and without limitation in chasing his dreams. And he never had to deal with the ultimate organization and disposition of the collections. An ideal situation for him—but not for those he left behind.

After his death, his lack of planning led to chaos. His widow was left wholly unprepared. Though she knew some of the dealers he had worked with, she knew little about the collections themselves. She had no way to evaluate them. None of his records and catalogues indicated what the items were worth. His correspondence with various museums was not definitive in stating where the items should go. Within months of his death, his widow was drowning in appraisers and appraisals. She spent weeks trying to prepare documents for estate tax returns and ultimately, gifts or sales.

Circled by dealers and auction houses and courted by museums eager to buy or accept various collections or items, she could not decide what to do. She grappled with unfinished purchases made before her husband's death and sorted out gifts he seemed to have committed to make. This had not been her choice, but she felt it was her responsibility to see it through. In the end, she discharged the collections heroically, but lost years to cleaning up her husband's dream—not chasing her own. "I have not had the freedom to enjoy the past two years of *my* life," she said to me, not without resentment.

Suppose, instead, the collector lived longer and had continued managing the collections, but still without a vision for their ultimate homes. As his memory weakened, he might have slowly lost track of items and their significance. His ability to discern what dealers and museums to trust could be compromised. If his mind started to slip, and he lost mental capabilities, he would have been completely overwhelmed by the details he once so easily recalled. He would have become miserable as he tried desperately to organize each collection and make each "perfect." He would likely have been completely exposed to unscrupulous advisors as well.

Although people may start collecting art or other tangibles when young, that collection usually grows as they age, especially if they have the wealth to support their passion. Even a small art collection—really just a few pieces—may become quite large with the passage of time. As people age, they are more and more eager to control their world, order it, and define themselves in terms of history and culture. For many, a well-managed collection can do all of that. If left unchecked, however, collecting can also become an obsession that takes over a person's life.

If you are an individual struck by such a passion—I am one myself—it's important to recognize any good collection has a beginning, a management phase, and an end. Preparing for that end is sometimes the hardest part for collectors. The beginning of a collection is easy. A collection starts with a spark—something that interests the collector. A wealthy graduate on a visit to Paris in the 1930s buys a Picasso. On a visit to Istanbul, a collector-to-be swoons over a lovely carpet and buys one . . . and then another . . . and another. Or the spark may be a small gift given by a spouse on their wedding day. It is rare for a collection to have an identifiable purpose or vision at the outset.

Every collector can recall when, where, and how their collecting began. But as acquisition follows acquisition and objects become numerous, and possibly valuable, collectors rarely, if ever, ask a key question: "What is this collection for?" And like the consummate collector just mentioned, they never consider, "What will happen when I'm gone?" You need to answer these questions, then establish strategies to manage your collections, both for yourself and those who will ultimately handle them. What starts as a wonderful hobby and pastime may evolve into a collection worth a sizable amount. Your stewardship of these objects—no matter what they are—must include identifying their ultimate resting place.

THE EVOLUTION OF A COLLECTION

As mentioned in Chapter 8, while in high school in 1964, I spent a summer living in Japan. As part of the Experiment in International Living—a student exchange program started in 1932 and still running strong today—I stayed with a Japanese family near Osaka. I had a Japanese "father," "mother," "brother," and two "sisters" with whom I lived. At the time, the country was preparing for its first Olympics since World War II. Holding such an event was intended to show the world that the country was returning to the community of peaceful nations. Although my Japanese father, like my real father, had fought in the war, he did not discuss it, other than to state that I must not visit Hiroshima.

During that summer, I fell in love with everything Japanese, and when I returned home that love only increased. (Distance does indeed make the heart grow fonder.) I searched out Japanese shops, food, and culture. A number of Japanese prints were actually brought to St. Louis by the Japanese government for the St. Louis World's Fair in 1904. I found that one of the established print shops in town specialized in Japanese woodblock prints (or *Ukiyo-e*), many of which had come out of people's attics sixty years after they were purchased at the World's Fair. I bought a few, all poor quality, but reminiscent of my time in Japan.

Over the years, my wife and I maintained close relationships with my "Japanese family," and my interest grew in Japanese prints. By 1980, the collecting "bug" really set in. My wife and I set out to find a number of *Ukiyo-e*. We looked for works by Hokusai, Hiroshige, and Utamaro—the unquestioned masters of the genre. Our expectations were extinguished by soaring prices, and, disappointed, we abandoned our quest. That is, until one day at a local print fair we saw a lovely triptych of soldiers looking at their reflections in a lake. The year depicted was 1894, and the soldiers had been fighting the Sino-Japanese War, Japan's first major overseas confrontation.

We bought the triptych, framed it, and returned annually to the print fair. Every year, we purchased similar triptychs of that war from the same dealer. Soon, other dealers found out about our interest and sought us out. As we acquired more prints, we set standards and expectations relating to condition, subject matter, and duplicates. With the help of numerous dealers, we began acquiring a quantity of prints and ephemera reflecting the rise of Japan as a military power from the mid-nineteenth century through World War II, with a special concentration on Japan's 1894 war with China and its 1904 war with Russia.

As the number of objects grew, it became harder to remember what we had and what we were looking for. We needed to better organize the pieces, and we wanted expert help to catalog and translate every print. We were ambitious enough to believe we should include scholarly information, such as the printer and engraver, as well as artist and subject. So, we hired a cataloger, an expert based in London. He came to our apartment two or three times a year cataloging, translating, and organizing. He used the information he organized and cataloged to connect with dealers, many of whom helped us add to our collection.

Our collection became known by dealers worldwide, so we had a constant stream of offerings coming to us. Often, a dealer in Tokyo would send us a picture of a print. If we knew we had that print in good condition and without any significant variations, we would turn down the offer. Within days, the same print would be offered by a dealer in San Francisco, and then a dealer in London. Prints were traveling around the globe going from dealer to dealer each of whom thought they could sell it to us. Our collection continued growing quickly.

As our objects became known, scholars and curators came to look at them. We found ourselves with guests for three or four days at a time, going through piles of prints at our dining room table. We had dedicated two of our closets—of which our apartment had too few—to store our woodblock prints. Our obsession was smothering us. Nevertheless, we did not want to quit chasing the unusual print or collection—we couldn't help ourselves! We continued buying several hundred prints each year. That was when a curator in a large European museum proposed that our pieces belonged in a museum, and his was willing to accept them. Shortly after, his offer was followed by a hint from the Smithsonian that the museum might be interested. We realized it was time to empty the closets and transform our acquisitions into a true collection.

As mentioned, any good collection has a beginning, a management phase, and an end. We'd already been through the "beginning" and the "management." Even as our acquiring continued, every item we collected was organized, listed, described, and cataloged. In the process, the entirety came to "make sense" as a collection. To truly move from disparate acquisitions to a collection requires a knowledgeable curator, and we ultimately felt we should turn to a museum with a strong curator. Our cataloguer's engagement continued throughout the acquisition stage. And now, we were considering museums.

After much deliberation, we chose our local museum. There, the Asian arts curator, who had actually helped us build the collection, worked with our cataloger to transition it to the museum. Over five years, a major exhibition, catalog, and book of essays were developed around the collection. The exhibition and volume were the final stage of turning our "collecting"— over 1,500 objects—into an actual collection. The exhibition opened with a symposium attended by scholars and collectors from around the world. My wife and I were thrilled to share all of our favorite pieces from over the years and to introduce experts to the genre, themes, and lessons of the works themselves.

The creation of that collection demanded help, and we could not have accomplished it alone. We had wonderful support from the museum, the curators, our cataloger, our dealers, and others. We reveled in the satisfaction of watching the collection blossom into something wonderful before our eyes. That wouldn't have happened if we simply donated the prints at our death or sent them to an auction house where they would be scattered to the winds. Importantly, we had a team, and everyone understood our goals and resources. Even as we lost some of the capacity to manage our growing number of prints, with the team's help, we progressed.

In effect, we had built the strategy to achieve our goals: To foster understanding of a country that went from a primitive island to the second most powerful military nation in the world, then to abject defeat only to re-emerge as the second most powerful economy in the world. With the pleasure of chasing objects and the great efforts of our cataloger, the curator, and the museum, our collection could serve its purpose of helping people better understand Japan, both past and present.

That purpose gave meaning to the time and energy we poured into our collection. And that meaning further contributed to our joy in finding and purchasing objects and in ensuring that the collection was well catalogued and ultimately well curated. If we hadn't understood what the collection was for, we wouldn't have enjoyed it in the same way. Maybe we would have lost interest and started looking for other items. But by answering the question, "What is the collection for?" and taking the proper steps to realize that purpose, we created and curated something we will forever be proud of.

WHAT IS THE COLLECTION FOR?

Just as you must identify what your wealth is for, you must decide what your collection is for. For many collectors, the answer just might be that acquiring and collecting are pleasurable and fun. There's nothing wrong with that. While some are more interested in the hunt, others find enjoyment in the collection itself.

Others aim to educate their community, invest for the future, or leave something tangible for their heirs. Thinking about the purposes of your collection will help you better understand your chase and choose the final destination of that collection. This exercise may come with a number of challenges, but once you fully explore those, you may reconsider why you're collecting in the first place. Ultimately, understanding the purpose of your collection allows you to better plan for its, and your, future.

THE THRILL OF THE HUNT

The joy of finding the exact piece you're missing. The satisfaction of a careful negotiation. Friendly (and sometimes not so friendly) competition with other collectors. New friendships. All of these elements contribute to the delight of collecting, which inspires many to start. An acquisitive zeal motivates such collectors. Rarely do they have excitement for the "dry" work of curating, detailed recordkeeping, analysis, and other less glamorous tasks necessary to creating a collection. For them, it's all about "the hunt." But ability to hunt can wane with age. Then what?

A famous rug collector I knew found himself in this exact situation. He had a beautiful collection from Turkey, Persia, and Russia. Every few months, he displayed three or four of them at a textile museum and spoke to an audience about each rug. He started each lecture by identifying the rugs and where and when they were made. Then, with stories worthy of movie archeologist Indiana Jones, he would tell of their acquisition: "I was in a bazaar in Tehran and a little boy came up to me, pulling on my shirt. 'Mister wait 'til you see what I just found you—come to my grandfather's house with me," and the story would go on.

When I got to know him, he had reached an age where he could no longer travel and scour exotic locales for additional pieces. The collections became dusty, even as his tales and stories got better. He still relished showing off the collection and reliving his experiences over and over. However, he never really curated his collection. Instead, at his death, it went to a museum that did the hard work of figuring out what he had, what was worth keeping, and how to catalog all of the pieces.

Wise collectors solely focused on the fun of the hunt should recognize that fact, but still keep *some* end in sight. If your collection is simply for the satisfaction and thrill of the hunt, it's even more imperative to determine the endgame. One of my favorite collectors was a Benedictine monk, a friend of mine who collected rare English literature books. The monk asserted that his vows did not include traditional poverty, so he set up a huge trust just before he entered the monastery. Thereafter, that trust funded purchases of multiple tomes. He amassed a huge collection as fine as any other. Indeed, he would take friends through the Morgan Library in New York, pointing out deficiencies in their collections that his could easily fill.

"Will you leave your collection to a library or museum?" I once asked him. "Oh no," he answered. "Once they are in a library or museum, I would have deprived others of the fun I had collecting them. After all, any one of them is available in paperback—Milton, Chaucer, Dickens. People will have no trouble finding copies to read. No, I will have them all sold, so that others can enjoy collecting them as I did." When he died, as directed in his will, the books were indeed all sold through a rare book dealer. Maximizing price was not the goal—distributing them was. The Benedictine monk's strategy ensured not just his own fun, but that of future book collectors as well.

ACTIVE ENJOYMENT

Some collections are intended to be actively used and enjoyed. Though this purpose can be part of a broader one, it can also be the purpose in and of itself. If that's the case, you must be crystal clear with your support team and loved ones; otherwise, they might not realize your intent. They may not even think of these items as a "collection" in the same way you do. For example, a woman I knew loved jewelry and had a fine collection. Every day, she selected a piece to wear, her fanciest reserved for certain galas and the simplest for daily use. She had two sons and often told them that her jewelry would be their inheritance. They didn't have much interest and planned to sell most of it off after she had passed away.

In her late nineties, though she didn't go out as much, she still enjoyed wearing pieces around the house, which she would spend hours meticulously matching and trying on. That activity was one of her most pleasurable daily routines until one day, at age ninety-nine, when she had a massive stroke. Her sons saw the jewelry as a good source of revenue to pay for her nursing care. "Easier than selling stocks and bonds and we'll end up reducing the insurance premium," said one. But, then one day she "woke up." Her miraculous recovery surprised everyone, including her doctors. Within days, she was ready to start wearing her jewelry. "Where are my rings, bracelets, and necklaces?" she asked. "I'd also love to put on my favorite brooch." Her sons had no choice but to tell her that they had sold it all off already (for more than $1 million). "I wanted to wear it, not sell it," she told them angrily. "How dare you sell my collection without my permission."

That woman lived another two years, and her sons did what they could to buy her some new pieces. How different her story would have been if she had planned strategically. Her jewelry was a "collection," but one to be enjoyed throughout her life and even into incapacity. On her death, it would belong to her sons, who could sell it as they saw fit, but during her lifetime it was hers to enjoy. Her sons, who themselves were of means, would never have sold the jewelry if that had been explicitly clear.

COMMUNITY EDUCATION

Another purpose of a collection can be to educate others, which usually requires building a strategy that results in curation, management, and placement in a museum. For example, consider a serial collector I know. He built a large collection in Meiji period Japanese woodblock prints, a narrow field at the time. Several venue museums held exhibitions he curated out of this collection, each with a different theme, and he wrote a book about each. Once he had introduced the world to the field through six or seven exhibitions and books, he gave the entire collection to the museum he believed would be the best stewards of the objects.

Then he started a new collection in a completely different area: engineering designs for vehicles. That collection also became the subject of exhibitions and books he authored before he gave it to a museum. And then he began another collection, in US primitives. And then *another* with a new focus, and so on. Each collection allowed him to continue writing and educating, giving him great satisfaction as he began to build his next one. Over and over, he educated communities by building, curating, sharing, and explaining each collection, then donating them.

Another successful example of an individual whose goal was educating the community was an art collector born and raised in St. Louis and educated in New England and Europe. Many years ago, he started a collection that contained works by many of the great artists of the nineteenth and twentieth centuries. He was selective and knowledgeable, and he added these pieces to the collection his parents owned. It resulted in one of the greatest private collections extant. In middle age, after the death of his first wife, he married a brilliant curator who knew art, but who also had extensive experience working with museums. She not only understood his collection but also the collections of various museums. She helped him figure out how to distribute various pieces to improve a museum's collection. Together, they planned where these pieces would end up.

After his death, she continued to purchase and collect. She began carefully promising works to different museums and universities. Each piece of art was deliberately paired with a museum or university that, in her analysis, "needed" it to flesh out or complete its publicly shown collections. In this way, she used the collection to build understanding for the good of the public, giving meaning to his and her passion for fine art. She was a collector and curator with an analytic understanding of museums and their roles in their communities.

LEGACY

Using a collection for legacy, typically in a museum, library, or university, requires forethought and careful analysis. That often includes a mastery of the collection itself and wise advisors to help implement a plan. Unlike the plan of our book collecting Benedictine monk, often that plan involves building legacy. That monk was not striving for legacy, but legacies can be created or burnished through great book collections. Consider some of the names that adorn famous libraries. The Morgan Library in New York City is forever associated with J.P. Morgan, the legendary financier and his phenomenal book collection. Other renowned book collectors whose names grace libraries across the country include Widener, Houghton, John Carter Brown, and Clemens. For them, the collection was only the beginning. As they aged, they and their advisors needed to think strategically about using the collections to build or enhance their legacy.

To do so, they needed to answer the following questions. If you plan to follow in their footsteps, you'll need to answer them as well:

- Where would the collection be located and shown?
- Will the collection or library be part of a university, say, Harvard or University of Michigan and ultimately rely on the University for funding and administration?
- If not, will it still be located on a University campus?
- Would it be placed in a dedicated room in an existing building, or would it be housed in a new building built by and named after the owner of the collection?
- In short, how would the collection be funded, used, and shown?

If a collection's primary purpose is legacy, it comes with its own set of challenges. A legacy museum can become a dead collection or mired in controversy. Consider the histories of the Isabella Stewart Gardner Museum or the Barnes collection. In the past, you may have believed once your name is attached to a collection—or is placed on a museum's façade—it is essentially eternal. Today, museum governance and collections are scrutinized based on the reputation or actions of the collectors (not just their collections). Collections themselves are examined and reexamined for relevance, provenance, and suitability by the day's standards. And when displayed, art and artifacts may be exposed in a new, public light and may result in a focus on the family name of the donor.

There have been instances of indigenous art in museums being returned to its indigenous creators. Pieces once taken from Holocaust victims have been returned to the victims' families. Many museums are facing new questions about, and criticism of, colonial art. Museums and collections attached to the Sackler fortune are considering whether and how to change their names. A bust of Avery Brundage, founder of the San Francisco Asian Art Museum, was removed from display in the museum after years of accusations that he was "a Nazi sympathizer and a racist."[4] Once your name is publicly attached to a collection, you bear the brunt of any controversy. Your actions, views, and deeds (or misdeeds) can overshadow the collection. There is no statute of limitations on what you may have done in the past and whether it can unravel your legacy.

There are other challenges when using a collection to burnish legacy. Consider the individual who gives a complete and significant collection to a museum to benefit posterity only to have the museum sell pieces to raise necessary operating funds. Such deaccessions were sanctioned for a two-year period starting in 2020 by the museum world to offset lost revenue form pandemic-driven closures. If that happens again, what is your legacy then? How can you build in safeguards, so your collection isn't sold off piecemeal to make ends meet for a struggling institution? Or suppose you give your collection subject to prohibition on a deaccession to a museum, but the museum sells much of its related material so yours does not have the context you intended. Then what? Careful consideration is clearly required if you intend your collection to be seen as your legacy.

FOR HEIRS

I frequently meet wealth holders who tell me their collection is for their heirs. They often say something like, "I am building a great art collection for my children and grandchildren." This sentiment sounds nice, but executing this intent raises many challenges and few, if any, benefits. A collection can be both a physical and financial burden. If you ask your heirs to keep your collection together as a "private collection" to be owned by the family, they must pay estate taxes equal to the *value of the collection*. In effect, they must buy your collection all over again.

If estate taxes are 50 percent, most would assume the tax on a $100 million dollar collection would be $50 million. But if your goal is to have your children keep the collection intact, the estate must have at least $100 million in other assets available to pay the tax on the total value of the collection and the other assets. Since that's the case, your estate must have a total of $200 million, $100 million of the collection and $100 million of the assets to pay the tax. In short, saving the collection for your heirs' enjoyment is expensive, and they will be stuck paying that cost.

A more significant challenge is that your heirs may not want to be the stewards or curators of your collection. If you've always focused on the fun of the hunt but then burden your children or grandchildren with the collection's upkeep after your demise, their resentment will hang over your gift. Making catalogs, engaging insurance and appraisal experts, finding places to store or hang the pieces, and ultimately deciding how to divide the collection at your death takes time, effort, and again, more money. Few inheritors will find satisfaction and self-actualization in curating a parent's collection, especially if they don't share the same interests as you.

Instead, encourage your heirs to start their own collections and find joy in their own pursuit. You'll all be better off if you do. Or rather than decreeing that your children keep the collection intact, turn your collection into cash and bequeath them the money. By treating the collection as an investment that needs to be maximized, you can still enjoy it throughout your life, and you leave heirs the means to build their own collections or the wealth to chase their own dreams.

FOR INVESTMENT

A collection can be a wise investment. Many objects purchased over the past fifty years have appreciated dramatically. Of course, many have not. And some have gone through continuous fluctuations. Consider a collection of a certain eighteenth-century porcelain, which was purchased for $700,000 in the eighties. By 2019, it was worth several million. Three years later, it was worth only $500,000. The collector was told, "No one wants it anymore."

If your collection is for investment, you need not find the museum or ultimate purchaser while you are acquiring pieces and objects. But you must develop an exit strategy ultimately to realize the collection's value. This strategy requires a market understanding of the collection, and markets are rarely static. Tastes and values change over time, sometimes quite drastically and quickly. Your strategy, therefore, needs to include a valuation process to maximize your financial return to account for the time and effort that went into the collection. It's not always easy, but if you are a successful "investor collector," you can turn a hefty profit.

Consider one of the world's foremost textile experts and dealers. A German gentleman, he started by finding and selling pieces of cloth, one at a time, to museums and other collectors. He soon recognized that selling a full collection of textiles would translate into considerably higher profitability. So, he started building collections in a deliberate and knowledgeable fashion. He carefully considered every element of each collection, strategically designing them with prospective purchasers in mind. His customers consisted of museums in the US, Europe, and Asia. For each collection, he found a museum, finished building the collection for that institution's specific needs, and then sold each for millions of dollars.

In the meantime, he was amassing his own collection of pianos and organs, an interest he began developing when he worked his way through college playing concerts on church organs in Alsace. With one of the largest collections of pianos and organs in the world, he designed his house in Switzerland to accommodate them. "Someday, I will have a museum for those musical instruments," he once told me. "My dream is to build a place where artists from around the world can entertain audiences and hear the beauty and versatility of these instruments."

After years of selling textile collections, he realized this dream. He recently sold a multi-million-dollar textile collection and moved his instruments into his new museum, which he built with the proceeds of that sale and others. His plan was being executed with the help of a museum curator, and a waiting list of musicians to play there is being created. He believes it will be the only museum like it in the world. His strategic thinking was that of a dealer who understood collecting. Yet, for his pianos and organs, he was a true collector—a dealer who never sells. His collection and museum would never have been possible without wisely investing in textile collections and understanding that market through and through.

A STRATEGIC PLAN

During your lifetime, you need to complete an actual plan for your collection. As you age the collection will require a road map and a strategy to guide it along that map. That plan is vital to ensure that collected objects follow a clear progression and the collection will be nurtured from its beginning, through its management, and to its end. Ideally, you will be there for every stage, but you will need help at each stage, particularly as you age and potentially become less interested in handling whatever stage the collection may be in. Your decision with respect to what the collection is for can help inform how the collection is built and how and where it ends. In other words, your decision can help you and your support team design the strategy.

If legacy or creating and sharing knowledge is the goal, the collection can be perfected most easily when the objects are given to a museum. The guiding hand of a curator can articulate how the objects fit together and help the collection make sense when it is shared with the world. If your collection should end in a museum, here are some of the questions to be answered in the strategy:

- How will the museum be selected?
- How will you be kept of the museum's evolving curatorial interest.

- What are the guidelines for disposition or deaccession? (Including instructions to govern when you are alive and after your death.)
- Do you want the museum to sell pieces it can't use, or would you prefer that you or your dealer or curator handle the sale or donation of such items?
- Is the collection a donation for "legacy" purposes?
- If the collection is for legacy purposes, will you want the gift named?
- How important is the tax deduction (whether you are alive or dead)?
- Do you want a catalog and opportunities for study—either through digital organization or facilitated research facilities?
- Should there be an endowment associated with the collection to fund scholarship?
- Will you want a catalog or scholarship associated with the collection?
- What information about your relationship with the collection should be part of the display and public recognition and who should design that?
- Like our Benedictine monk, is your true goal to ensure that others share in the pleasure you have enjoyed?

If your collection is for investment or, like the Benedictine monk's, for ultimate disposal, you do not need to find an ultimate purchaser right away, but you do need to keep the markets in mind and be familiar with potential buyers. As shown with the textile collector, if you want to treat your collection as an investment, such knowledge is paramount.

If your collection is to be ultimately sold, a detailed inventory of capable dealers will be important. If investment is your purpose, a critical part of your plan is deciding when to sell—before or after your death—and who will sell it. That process should first include an evaluation of your collection and a determination if some strategic purchases are necessary to increase its value. Ask yourself, "Should the items be sold piecemeal or as a collection?"

Regardless of the plan, as suggested throughout the chapter, any large collection demands hard work to maintain and position it for the future. Careful records about their ownership, provenance and cost must be maintained. The pieces must also be identified and easy to locate. For planning purposes, a valuation can also be extremely helpful. Again, don't be shy about seeking professional advice. Working with catalogers, curators, and honest dealers, you'll ensure the collection ends up in a place that will make you proud.

A number of years ago, one wealth holder was lamenting about the future of his prized collection. "I don't know how my wife will sell the collection, since she doesn't know the market and what dealers to use," he told me. "Neither she nor my children are interested in it. They will be taken advantage of!" I observed that his concern could be met by selling the collection during his lifetime. If he were to sell it himself, he would certainly get the top dollar. The capital gains tax could be offset by the higher price, and the cash might even be moved into a trust to avoid estate tax on the appreciation. Yet, this collector was not ready to quit collecting. "What shall I do?" he asked me.

At my suggestion, he started with a cataloger, an academic expert in the field, twenty years his junior. Together, they spent time working to understand every item in the collection: Where and how it was purchased; where and how it would make sense to sell; and what was the most opportune time to sell. They created a timeline based on the acquisitions that would round out the collection, so it would be of maximum interest and value to another collector. This wealth holder could now rest assured that the collection would be sold for what it was worth. After he died, his family and trustees relied on the cataloger to arrange a successful sale to another collector at the kind of lofty price only another collector would pay. Had that cataloger not been there to drive the sale, the family would have been entirely lost.

A less successful result ended the collection of a collector who relied on one dealer his own age to build a "priceless" collection of objects worth many millions. The collector had cataloged the collection, and he and the dealer were in constant communication. The collector fully intended to sell the collection when the objects were their most valuable, but he became unable to understand the collection as he aged. It simply gathered dust until his death. His widow wrote to the dealer in Europe to ask for help in selling the collection, but the dealer had died, and his successor wrote back that the objects were no longer in demand. "As objects, they can be donated to thrift stores" was her message to the widow. "No one wants these old-fashioned things at this time, but they may come back into style someday." Without a strategy designed during his lifetime, that collection lost all of its financial value.

Whether you are alive, incapacitated, or dead, someone has to carry out your plan. Whom have you chosen for this role? Does that person understand the plan enough to execute it well? That can only happen if you have discussed these matters with that person or those to serve as your support team. The team needs to include someone who understands you *and* the collection. If you have been working with someone—perhaps a cataloger or curator—for a number of years, they will likely become a strong member of your team. Dealers can also be a good addition to the team, so long as you have confidence in their integrity. Support will become increasingly important as you age, and the collection grows.

CONCLUSION

Building and developing a collection can be one of life's great joys. But if you become a serious collector and your works of art, ephemera, or other objects grow into a substantial collection, you'll need to consider the purpose of that collection. There's no one correct "purpose" behind a collection, and sometimes a number of purposes can be in place together, or one after another. Indeed, the fun of the hunt, your intellectual enjoyment, enlightenment and education of a community, legacy enhancement, and valuable investment are not mutually exclusive purposes. But each purpose has its challenges, and regardless of the purpose of the collection, strategy is required, particularly as you age. That strategy requires that you resource and rely on professionals to help you properly manage, curate, and ultimately place or dispose of the collection when the time is right.

CHAPTER 12
MEMBERSHIPS: ENGAGING WITH CIVIC AND SOCIAL COMMITMENTS

As a young lawyer, I once stayed at one of the most exclusive clubs in New York City. Over lunch, the club was filled with active business executives discussing deals, politics, and the news of the day. But by 2:00 pm, such conversations were done. In fact, talk of any kind had almost entirely ceased. A quiet calm hung over the library and halls, which were then full of the old lions of Wall Street dozing in large, overstuffed chairs. There they sat and slept until dinner, or until someone took them home. In several cases, it was difficult to know whether they were dead or alive. Meanwhile, staff patrolled the halls to catch the occasional mess that comes with incontinence.

I haven't stayed there since. Now I just go for lunch, when the place is guaranteed to be filled with young, active members—but I often wonder why these old men still go there day in and day out and remain dues paying members (possibly on dues reduced by reason of age). Perhaps they have told their wives and children they're transacting business (and maybe those very same wives and children are delighted to have them out of the house). Or it is possible that the sense of familiarity and comfort they get from the club are well worth the membership dues The club might even provide them with some level of care during the day. It has never been quite clear to me. What is clear is that those lions probably don't want to be remembered by Wall Street as some tired old men, slouching in those chairs, sleeping away the afternoon. It can't be good for the lions' image or for the club's environment and reputation.

But whose duty is it to help these men? Should the club evaluate the members based on their age and executive function? Or should they relocate those comfortable chairs to a less visible area? Maybe eliminate them altogether? Whether the club considers these former captains of industry its responsibility or urges them to spend their afternoons there (spending their money over lunch), someone should ask these gentlemen if this is how they want to be remembered.

Memberships—whether in social clubs and groups, churches or religious associations, charities, health clubs, or otherwise—are often central to the life of a vibrant, active person. As that vibrancy diminishes, you need to consider if you'd like to maintain involvement in those clubs and associations. Over a lifetime, they have likely become important to you in any number of ways, but how you use them requires objective analysis as you age. If they are not strategic in terms of your needs, the associations themselves may become detrimental to your well-being.

In many ways, reconsidering your memberships relates to a foundational question as you become less competent: What do you want to do with your days? What are you willing to spend or sacrifice to maintain an industrious façade? You likely want to stay "active," (whatever that means), but do you want to end up publicly "inactive?" Does snoring in a Lay-Z-Boy while younger members of "your" club tiptoe past you enhance your legacy? These questions are at the heart of how you approach memberships as you get older. You may want to stay involved, but only up to a point. Or you may determine you can't do without the social connections and familiarity, no matter your state of mind or body. Either way, it's important to dedicate time to thinking about these memberships and their importance in your life. To start, let's look at the groups you may be involved in and how that involvement might be affected as you age.

SOCIAL CLUBS AND GROUPS

When considering social clubs and groups, whether a country club or a city or university club, you must balance the comfort of your habits against the discomfort those habits might impose in old age. A woman I know unfortunately aged without thinking about this balance. Her father-in-law was the founder of one of the most prominent country clubs in her town. Her husband had once been president. Almost every summer afternoon, she and her husband went to the club together to swim, play tennis and golf, and dine with friends. As they aged, they continued using the club all the time. They even had their favorite table in the "Grill Room," where they regularly entertained friends or enjoyed a quiet meal together. After her husband died, she had a "widow's membership," and she visited the club almost every day, mostly to take friends to dinner and eat at "her" table. As she reached ninety, she began to suffer dementia. At ninety-three, she recognized no one.

She had always wanted to continue to stay in her apartment, so her children, who lived out of town, arranged for twenty-four-hour caregivers. In accordance with their mother's wishes, these caregivers were asked to always wear uniforms and nurse caps, to which they agreed. Every night, the woman and her "nurse" went to the club, sat at her favorite table, and ate dinner. Other members stopped by to say hello, but her dementia had become full blown at that point. Even though she did not recognize them, she still spoke cordially. As she aged further, however, she became less communicative.

The nightly dinner at the club was pricey, particularly given the fact she ate only a few bites of her meal—always a steak and a baked potato—and club membership was expensive as well. Her two children wondered whether they should cancel her membership and instead have one of the caregivers prepare dinner every night. After all, it was hard to imagine that her mother really understood the membership and experience. But her children could never bring themselves to do so.

The woman lived to be 100 years old, spending her final years without any apparent cognitive capacity. She also spent the last five years of her life having dinner every night at her favorite table at her club with her "nurse," eating a bite of that steak and a spoonful of her baked potato. Since her children couldn't be with her, they never heard the other club members who complained about their mother's condition. In fact, other members began avoiding the Grill Room during the hour or two their mother and the caregiver ate dinner there, perhaps because of embarrassment or perhaps because the old woman reminded them of the condition that might affect them before long.

It was too bad the woman's children never discussed her priorities about the club before her dementia set in. At age sixty-five, she could have considered what she would have truly wanted and the ramifications and embarrassment of losing her executive function on such a public stage. The children could then have weighed the gain from taking dinner every night at the club against the inadvertent downsides she and her reputation would suffer. It's possible she would have felt comfortable eating in the club no matter what her age or mental state. Maybe she would have always been willing to sit at the same table with a uniformed "nurse." Or maybe she would have found this mortifying. With her declining cognitive capacity on display for all to see—undermining her reputation and relationship with the club—she may have preferred to stay at home. But the children did not have that conversation. Instead, they erred on the side of their mother's "comfort." Unfortunately, their mother, who was a dignified and prominent member of the club, became an embarrassment to everyone—an outcome she unlikely ever foresaw or desired.

On the other hand, some social clubs act as a support center for their members as they age. In contrast to the New York club full of somnambulant former Wall Street titans, another club—not in New York, not as prominent, and not as full of lions—deliberately avoids big, soft, easy chairs. Instead, it has an upper floor in the club with "restrooms." These small rooms, each with a single bed, are set aside for old men after lunch for a "rest." The rooms are staffed by attendants who change sheets and pillows as needed. The old men can sleep in privacy and everyone seems happy with that arrangement. And they can go home at night to tell their families they had a busy day at "the office." Perhaps that alone is worth the price of membership and the modest daily charge for the room.

CHURCHES OR RELIGIOUS ASSOCIATIONS

Membership in a religious community often defines an individual's identity. Remaining a member of a particular community until your death may be very important to you. Or you may decide to join or change congregations for one reason or another. Some continue to belong to a certain congregation specifically to ensure that there will be "someone who knows me to bury me." Others switch for the very same reason, finding a different pastor or religious leader that they are more comfortable with to oversee their funerals. Certainly, if you move to a new city, state, or country—or even move in the same town but have a harder time getting to your place of worship—you might consider switching your affiliation. Another possibility is that as your family grows, and your children give you grandchildren or otherwise, the center of your religious orientation may shift. You may want to change your place of worship to accommodate their lives and your family unity.

My parents, for example, were raised in an established Reform Jewish Temple. Their parents were members as well, maintaining a relationship with the congregation's beloved Rabbi for many years. Yet, when my parents had children, they wanted a smaller, more intimate congregation and joined nineteen other families in starting a new Temple. That Temple—with a then-young Rabbi—would become the religious home for my parents and for me. I even served as President of the congregation. But what about the relationships with the old Temple and its aging Rabbi? My living grandparents were in their seventies when the new Temple was founded. They wanted to become part of the new religious community their children had chosen. They looked forward to attending services with their children and grandchildren and developing a relationship with the young congregation and its Rabbi. However, they still felt fondness and loyalty to the aging Rabbi in the old congregation.

As a type of compromise, my parents and grandparents decided to keep memberships in both Temples. They thought of the new temple as their congregation, but the aging Rabbi remained their friend and counselor for some purposes. It was crucial to my grandparents that they not desert him. He actually died before any major lifecycle events took place in the family—funerals, marriages, and so forth. So, they never had to decide where such services would be held, in the old congregation or the new. Ultimately, as they aged, they found satisfaction in keeping both memberships so long as the old Rabbi lived. When the old Rabbi died, my grandparents and parents gave up their membership in his Temple.

You may end up in a similar situation. What you felt was right for yourself may not be the same for your children, or grandchildren. As you age, you might want to remain close to your family's religious practices—which are part of both their spiritual and social lives—without leaving behind long-standing relationship with groups, congregations, or religious leaders you've come to cherish. The benefit of maintaining memberships in both new and old congregations is that you enjoy the best of both worlds. Your family can transition gracefully between congregations without your losing your connection to a beloved congregation or pastor.

However, children who leave their parents' congregations often "make" their aging parents follow. The parents—long seen as respected members of the congregation where they raised children—join their family elsewhere. They cease being long-term, solid members of the old congregation, becoming instead "the parents of" their children in a new one. If membership is primarily about life events, there is logic in that decision: Children will be the major participants in the funeral of a widowed parent. But if your membership is about community and feeling part of what you have helped build over many years, that choice may not make sense. The decision of where to maintain membership is more complicated than simply "following" your children, and it is one you must make for yourself. Talk to your family now about what you'd like for your future involvement in your congregation. Discuss various implications if you were to switch and the meaning of such a change. And if you want to stay a member in your current church, temple, mosque, or other place of worship, make that perfectly clear. Don't leave it up to your children, who may think it's in your best interest to "lift" you out of your old community and place you in a new one. As you get older, you'll want to be comfortable in the knowledge that you're a member of the congregation that will best serve your spiritual needs and desires.

CHARITIES

Of lesser importance, but often critical, are various member-ships in charitable circles. This includes membership in a college society, a museum, or a political support group. Many have a string of these memberships and become regular contributors to any number of charities. When you are alert and your executive function is fully intact, you can maintain those memberships through annual gifts. But if your executive function starts to slip, management of your charitable program can become quite difficult. For example, a dowager client of ours made annual gifts to over 100 local charities: those she had been involved with through board membership and leadership; those her friends asked her to give to; those for which a solicitation had caught her eye; and those to which she "had always given."

As she entered her nineties, she could no longer keep track of the solicitations and all of the checks she had written. She found herself ignoring some charities and giving twice to others. Aware that she was having trouble, charities started sending solicitors to her home. "We will only ask once annually," said one fundraiser (though he was asking for the second time that year). And as she received multiple mail solicitations, she gave three or four gifts per year when she only intended one.

Her advisors became concerned, so they set up a process: She deposited all the solicitations in a shoe box. Then, four times a year, she and her advisors went through the box together. They kept "score" on notecards and spreadsheets. With each request, and with the aid of the advisors, she could plan out her charitable giving for the year. Decisions became more consequential as she began to commit substantial funds to two or three charities. She wanted to be sure she had enough for them without depleting the charitable funding she already committed to a number of organizations. Yet, it was important to her to stay philanthropically involved, both because she believed it the right thing to do with her wealth and as part of her image in her community. The disciplined process her advisors designed enabled her to do just that well past the age where she could do it all casually or alone.

Though such memberships can be well worth your time and energy, as you get older, you need a system in place to manage them. This can be as simple as the shoe box approach or something more formal—whatever works for you and your advisors. Whether that system is devised by you when you were capable or later with your support team, it needs to be clear, easy-to-use, and readily available no matter your age. Before you put such a system in place, your team must understand the organizations and causes you want to support. You need to proactively communicate the overall goals of your giving, so they will be honored by your heirs and advisors. This kind of clarity will avoid the debacle I've seen before—donations with no discernible strategy, or with loss of prominence in community or a charitable organization or that violate the wealth holders' wishes.

A failure to clearly communicate your strategy to your loved ones or your team can create difficulties for your family. This is exactly what happened to a very generous businessman I knew. He had created a very large, charitable foundation that he named after his wife and himself. "This is *our* foundation," he repeated over and over. In fact, he made all the major decisions. In their names, the foundation committed substantial sums for endowments, academic chairs, and building improvements, all to charities on whose board the husband had served. He would allocate smaller gifts to charities on whose boards the wife had served, but it was clear that the foundation was meeting *his* vision, focusing on *his* interests. Then he died unexpectedly.

Shortly after his death, the last of his large pledges was paid. Suddenly, the widow was now obligated under the tax laws to distribute millions of dollars each year to charities she was required to select. She was without direction and had no understanding about her husband's desires. Relatively young, she went through a difficult emotional process considering how to continue the foundation grants. Should she simply honor her husband by making huge gifts to each of his charities, possibly exhausting the foundation entirely, but preserving and enhancing further his legacy in the community? Or should she develop her own interests, nurturing charities in which she wanted to be more involved? Because she had never discussed these options with her husband, the decision became entirely hers. She was torn between what she really wanted to do and the guilt of not knowing and honoring what he would have wanted.

Two years after her husband's death, she began the process of deciding how *she* would be remembered in the community. She also considered how she might engage her children and grandchildren in her philanthropic efforts. She repurposed the foundation, so it reflected her role in the community and her role in the family. She focused on organizations *she* had been involved with over the years. This thoughtful approach allowed her to define her legacy in the community. She set up funds for her children and grandchildren to distribute and created processes to engage them in giving back to their communities as well. The foundation would no longer simply be a tribute to her deceased husband but would instead become "theirs" and their family's.

During her husband's life, they spent many hours talking about estate planning, and they had written numerous wills and trusts. But there had never been much attention devoted to the future of the foundation. He always said they could work on that later. That part of their planning—or failure to plan—left the widow without any direction over the foundation's future after one of them had died. Those considerations should have been as important as their plans for passing their private wealth to their children.

A WASTE OF MONEY?

All too often, trustees, children, and support teams decide that charity memberships and regular charitable gifts are "wasted money" without real value to an aged wealth holder. Unilaterally, they stop them. Yet, in many cases, it would be better that those gifts continue, so the wealth holder can remain involved with the organizations in some way. Technically, this can be done through deferred giving, charitable foundations, and provisions in a will. But often the gifts that are important to these groups are those memberships in the $500 to $5,000 range. These can be hard to institutionalize, even while you are competent to do so.

You can provide for annual charitable amounts in your revocable trust, so your traditional gifts and memberships can continue even after your incapacity. It may be equally necessary to explain to your foundation directors and your own trustees the ongoing memberships and annual gifts most important to you. There may be board seats that require minimum annual gifts. You may want to continue qualifying for those seats regardless of your health. All of these decisions require careful planning long before you get older and start losing any executive function.

Through her gifts to a major institution in her town, a widow became friendly with the director. He visited her regularly. Although she liked to think of the visits as social—over dinner, cocktails, or coffee—he used them to solicit her. She enjoyed these get-togethers and always followed up with an annual gift. Then one day over dinner he suggested she donate millions of dollars to fund an endowment, the proceeds of which would fund a pet project of his.

She said she would need to think it over. She then called

me to ask for my advice. "If I make this sizeable contribution, I won't be giving again to that charity," she told me. I asked whether if she quit giving to the charity, the visits from the director would stop. She thought they might. So, she and I designed a plan whereby she would give an amount each year that would have been the "harvest" from the endowment gift requested. Thereafter, the director regularly called on her to assure that annual gift. She left the charity the endowment amount by will and never lost the pleasure of his annual visit, his company, during her lifetime. Her planning worked to maintain the association she so enjoyed. At the same time, she gave the charity what it needed from an endowment. Everyone benefitted. It would be hard to argue that her donations were a "waste of money," for her or the organization.

How often the attention that widow and others are looking for in old age comes from engagement in a charitable project. Once that involvement stops—either because a large "last time" gift is made or because trustees decide that with the donor incapacitated, the gifts would be a waste of money—the attention and pleasure ends. How much better to continue the gifts and stretch them out over the donor's remaining lifetime.

Health Clubs and Gym Memberships

Finally, it's worth mentioning health clubs and gym memberships. These facilities may seem unnecessary when you are no longer so active, but they can remain an important resource for relaxation and socializing. You may not be playing tennis or golf anymore, but you may still want a regular massage, steam bath, or jacuzzi soak. A friend of mine suffering from Parkinson's disease is taken daily to his health club, where he has some physical therapy, and most importantly, a half hour steam.

I belonged to a downtown club that was well known for its athletic facilities. It had exercise equipment, a steam bath, and a pool. For many years, it was a men's-only club. I used to go early in the morning for a cardio workout, followed by a steam and shower. Every morning, seven or eight elderly men limped into the locker room, removed their clothes (the pool prohibited bathing suits), and slid into the pool, often with the help of attendants. Afterward, those men went into the steam room where they either dozed or talked about football, baseball, and other topics.

In time, there was a proposal to allow women to join the club. Businesses in the community had been threatening to boycott the establishment because of its discriminatory policy and, simply put, times were changing. It was clear the policy had to change, too. But there were those old men. And there were many of them. A number of them threatened to quit.

One day, four of them came out of the pool and into the steam room. They were excitedly and disapprovingly reviewing the proposal. I was in the steam room, too, admittedly as a much younger man, but I was welcomed to join in their outrage at the possibility that women might be admitted to the club. "It would be outrageous," said one. "How would we swim if we had women members?" I observed that their options would be not to swim, to wear a bathing suit, or to continue to swim nude (though the women would not). None of those solutions seemed ideal to the old men. One got even more excited: "What if I am on a treadmill"—I had never seen him on one—"and I start to sweat! That would certainly be a problem if a woman was working out next to me." I pointed out that she might sweat, too, but he did not seem to think my observation was relevant.

In the end, women were admitted to the club, and the pool

changed its rules to allow bathing suits. As far as I know, those old men never started using the treadmills, so they never had to worry about sweating in front of female patrons. They did continue to use the steam room (the women had their own) and their discussions of football, baseball, and other "weighty" matters of the day. They paid dearly in dues considering their only use of the club became the steam room. But they didn't mind, and the changes at the club did not affect their membership. In fact, by admitting women, the club ensured its own survival, so that those old men could spend their mornings there.

As they aged, like many people, these men sought continuity and companionship. They could find both in the club, and they valued that. They felt threatened by the club's admission of women, in part, because they saw it as a break in that continuity and a threat to their companionship. After all, the club was less of a place they went to exercise, and more of a place they went to socialize. Yet without women, that club would have had to close. Ultimately, those old men got most of the continuity they wanted—and continued their friendships—as the club modernized.

CONCLUSION

Memberships can be a boon or a burden—and sometimes both—as you age. They can provide comfort in old age but they can also threaten your reputation. They can provide a place to gather with friends and family, or to stay involved in causes you'd like to support financially. Your relationship with various organizations—social, religious, charitable, health, or otherwise—may change over time, but you need to make sure those changes take place on your terms. Talk to your support team, family, and advisors about your different memberships and how you'd like to manage them. You may decide that some are less desirable (or even harmful) if you start losing executive function, while others may be more desirable as you look for comfort and social companionship. Clearly define the level of involvement in those groups, clubs, and charities most important to you, and in those you may want to give up. Whatever you choose, make sure your decisions are clear and right for you.

CHAPTER 13
THE FINAL ACT: OBITUARIES, FUNERALS, AND LEGACY

A friend of mine was a successful theatrical producer. Though he also made some movies and television shows, his true love was live theater. On his seventieth birthday he told me, "I am now entering the final act, call it Act Five. It is time to prepare for the close of this play by staging the curtain call and making sure the *Times* gives me a good review." I smiled—he'd always been dramatic. He started planning his funeral—who would speak, what music would be played, where it would be, and who would officiate. He dreamt up a post-funeral celebration as well—"a cast party without the producer." Then he jotted down notes for his obituary, preparing for his "review." Every aspect was perfectly choreographed. Alas, he died during Covid, and his funeral and cast party could not take place. But the obituaries were brilliant.

The ultimate aging event is death. Even those elderly men and women among us who are fond of saying "if I die"—and refuse to say "when I die"—will in fact succumb to that grim reaper. As you age, you will likely attend more funerals than you would like, realizing at each that you are closer to your own grave. How you approach those funerals is, of course, up to you—with a sense of sadness and morbidity for the loss of a friend or loved one, joy and celebration of the life led, or humor and wit to make it all easier. Whenever my father's mother would attend a graveside funeral, she would say wryly, "Why not just leave me here to wait for my own?" Whenever my father attended a funeral, he would wonder why he was there, saying "after all, they won't be attending mine."

Maybe you've become a dedicated reader of the obituary columns, often seeing names you recognize or people you knew, many of whom were your contemporaries. Or perhaps you can't remember whether a friend or celebrity is alive or dead. Maybe at your most recent check-up your doctor told you, "Don't worry about it. At your age, you will more likely die of something else." In other words, you may spend more and more time ruminating about death, when it will come, and what it will look like.

We naturally start contemplating death as we get older. We may picture our funeral, wondering who will be there, who will perform the eulogy, and what will be said about us. We ask ourselves, will anyone even show up? What about logistics if Covid cases spike again or we're plagued by another pandemic? Will there be a subsequent "celebration of life" instead of a traditional funeral? We also think about our friends and family, and how they will be reminded of our lives and accomplishments. We might even start writing our obituary. In summary, we think about how we will be remembered and honored and what our legacy will be.

There is no harm in musing about this "final act," but if your burial and obituary are important to you, it is best to start planning while you are young enough to think them through fully. It is not easy to script a funeral or an obituary on your death bed. Both will be part of how you solidify your legacy.

THE OBITUARY

In his middle age, my dear friend the Benedictine monk, started keeping a yellow legal pad in his desk drawer on which he was drafting his obituary. Twice a year—on his birthday and his half birthday—he took out the pad and modified the latest version. As a student of literature, his obituary included quotes from many of the books he loved, and he closed with a passage from the Bible. With every passing year, that obituary got longer. He enjoyed writing that "final note," embracing the solitary solemnity and formality it involved. Penning it over the years allowed him to examine his own mortality and accomplishments, providing him with an opportunity for introspection.

Though it may not be for everyone, by writing your own obituary, you dedicate time to reflect on your life and legacy. Insight is likely to follow, especially in how you want to be remembered or place yourself in "history." In that way, you can control your final narrative, as opposed to leaving it up to someone else. Even as a "dead hand," you will be able to influence how posterity remembers you. Moreover, it can also be a pleasurable experience, as it was for my friend the monk, confronting death with the consolation of a life well lived.

For those of you working on your own obituary, you can find some stellar examples of good obituaries in the work of Alden Whitman, the distinguished writer of obituaries for *The New York Times* from 1964 until 1976. Many believe Whitman perfected the art of obituary writing in the United States. He started every obituary during the lifetime of the subject, and a call from Mr. Whitman with a request for an interview meant you would likely be memorialized in the *Times*. Those interviewed had a chance to consider how they would like to be remembered. The obituaries were kept up to date until the subject's final moment, so they could be published within several days of the individual's death. The published obituaries were read carefully by the subject's friends and by readers who learned social history through the lives of the deceased. However, if you want to control what is written about you, don't leave it all up to reporters, who may never even interview you.

A model different from Whitman's is the model of the *Times* of London. After college, a friend of mine landed a job there, and as a young reporter, he was assigned to write obituaries. Unlike the American style of immediate, post-death publication, the London paper waited until death and then assigned this young reporter to study the deceased's life. There was no rush at all to publish the sometimes long and involved obituaries. After all, the deceased would remain deceased in perpetuity. As a result, these obituaries were carefully researched and much less likely to reflect the individual's desire for what should be written—the deceased could not be interviewed for the piece.

It's also important to recognize that obituaries are no longer the art they once were. Indeed, some papers don't bother printing them at all, though they may sell space to families who would like to have the deceased's obituary published in small print. As fewer and fewer journalistic obituaries are published by local papers, those paid obituaries have gotten longer and longer. Going well beyond death notices, they often have pictures of the deceased, with detailed explanations of their accomplishments and love for their family. Though the obituary has become a lost art, the upside here is that, if you write your own while you're alive, your family can have it printed or placed online after your death. Don't be surprised if they embellish it (and let's hope for the better).

Ultimately, whether you write your own obituary, or someone writes it for you, your life should dictate its content. And no matter your choice, don't fret over it too much. Without the Alden Whitmans of the world, your memory is unlikely to be preserved solely by an obituary. What will truly preserve your memory is how you lived. From time to time, when you want to feel mortal, open the obituary page of your paper. Read the parade of names and stories, news of whose death rarely lasts for more than a few days. Unless you are a celebrity or criminal, your obituary will likely be little more than a footnote to your life.

THE LEGACY BOOK OR VIDEO

If you would like something written about your personal history that will likely have a longer shelf life than a newspaper obituary, you may want to consider a more involved project—a "legacy book" or "legacy video." One of these chronicles of your life can be an important element of your legacy, shared with your family for generations after you're gone. Such books or videos, which could be produced by you or a family member (with or without a professional's help), detail your accomplishments throughout your life. They are an opportunity to highlight stories, experiences, and advice you'd like to pass on to your children, grandchildren, and others. These works should not be didactic. Instead, you want to show readers or viewers why your life was worth living, leading them to contemplate their own. Many of these works have helped establish a person's legacy in meaningful ways for the family and the community.

For example, as mentioned in Chapter 9, a granddaughter of a previously unknown, though major, figure in the Manhattan Project wrote a book about her grandfather's role. At the time, his story had been pretty much lost. His duties had been top secret, so he received no recognition for his incredible work. But his granddaughter secured his place in history, along with that of his team, when she wrote a legacy book about him. A detailed, well-conceived account, the book brought light to his many achievements. In doing so, she not only preserved her grandfather's legacy, but actually enhanced it.

Journals and diaries can also be used as a type of legacy book even after a person is gone, giving life to a subject and securing an individual's place in history. Jacob Nagle, an American sailor who circumnavigated the globe during and after the American Revolution, kept a detailed journal during his travels. If it weren't for that journal, his adventures would have been entirely forgotten. Author John Dann transformed the recollections of this intrepid explorer into *The Nagle Journal: A Diary of the Life of Jacob Nagle, Sailor, from the Year 1775 to 1841*, giving the journal wider circulation and educating future generations.

Unfortunately, too often these legacy books and videos are about "how I got rich and how rich I got." That's almost the exact working title of one book a client of mine was writing. He considered himself the perfect model of "rags to riches," pleased he had built and sold a huge business that ensured generations of rich offspring. When we discussed the book, I asked him if he expected all of his children and grandchildren to replicate what he had done, making themselves and their descendants many times richer. His first response was that he wanted them to understand how he had benefitted them and why it was important to preserve the wealth he had created. With that information, I understood what he truly wanted: To help his descendants become "family wealth stewards," effectively the curators of his "wealth collection."

With that realization in mind, I started a discussion with him about his accomplishments, first focusing on how he built his wealth. As a young man, he had been practically homeless, sleeping in his car and uncertain of his path forward. But even then, he realized the world was becoming more global. What might be popular in Woolworth's in Los Angeles could be manufactured in China. With hard work, lots of travel and an understanding of human nature that transcended cultures, he built a large import-export business. And in the process, he became wealthy beyond his dreams.

The lessons in his story reflect the qualities he hoped his own offspring would cultivate. These included perseverance in the face of adversity and courage to reconsider one's options and capabilities when daily life was a struggle. He believed in being guided by a vision of the world and chasing that vision to make it real. In other words, he wanted to communicate that through thick and thin, he had pursued self-actualization, and every reader of his book should, too. His accomplishment was not actually getting rich, but how he led his life and chased his dream. His legacy book ended up with a title that conveyed that larger message.

By creating such a legacy book or video, you can leave something concrete behind to inform future generations. This long-form piece is much more effective than an obituary, a final will and testament, or a hope that people will remember what you have taught them through your personal and professional successes. A legacy piece gives you the dedicated opportunity to look back on your life and share all of the wisdom you've gained through your unique, lived experiences. If you truly care how you will be remembered, these books and videos are an excellent way to frame, and even improve, your legacy.

THE FUNERAL

Even if you don't pen your obituary, write a legacy book, or produce a video about your life, as you think about your funeral, it is not unreasonable to ask yourself, "What do I want my funeral to accomplish?" As with all of the most critical questions you must answer with aging, you should consider this one while you're still competent and sharp. For some, a funeral is merely a nice occasion where people gather to think fondly of you, then leave and return to daily life. For others, it may be an opportunity to build family ties and possibly mend broken fences, even from beyond the grave. If it's meant to restore family harmony—without testing family members' patience—some opt for an intimate ceremony with a trusted pastor at a grave.

A friend of mine wanted just such a funeral. His brother and sister were estranged from each other, but both got along with him. He hoped his funeral might be an occasion where some peace could be restored between them. As he described the plans to his wife and Rabbi, he told them that all he truly wanted was to bring the family together. His wife would give a luncheon, including his brother, sister, and their children. All of these plans were decided years before his death. When the time came, the funeral was sentimental, and the luncheon provided an opportunity for everyone to reminisce. His wife and Rabbi encouraged communication among the estranged family members, and they all shared in a small celebration of my friend's life. In the end, my friend's plan worked: thereafter, his brother and sister were willing to communicate civilly.

Wakes, visitations, and other receptions can bring together people not only to reminisce, but also to start building new relationships and plans, making the funeral a quasi-business event. Though the primary function may not be to swap business cards or add connections to attendees' LinkedIn profiles, if your work was a big part of your life, you may encourage people to mingle and connect on a professional level. In this way, you're providing value to your colleagues and network one last time. Maybe some former associates can start new relationships. And fences may be mended among business associates or partners as well. After all, it is difficult to fight at a wake (though it has been done).

A well-conceived funeral can also be a chance for your next generation to display leadership in the community. The funeral service can spotlight heirs by placing them by the side of your widower or widow. Or they can deliver eloquent eulogies. Similarly, it can also emphasize the impact of your business to an heir apparent or motivate former employees with your words of wisdom. I know one wise fellow who published a book of his sayings to be distributed at his funeral. Perhaps the most famous funeral oration was Mark Antony's, as presented by Shakespeare. Prior to that oration, the crowds favored Brutus and the others who had assassinated Caesar. Antony's speech used emotion to win over the crowd. Although great drama, such a well-designed funeral can indeed sway passions, provide lessons, and introduce successors, all of which add to your legacy.

No matter what you want to accomplish with your funeral, it should be designed with your end goal in mind. That goal may not be served by a traditional religious funeral and that fact might enter into your planning. Most religious ceremonies are intended to console survivors and nurture the grief that comes with the death of a loved one. There is a certain comfort in a traditional ceremony that has been followed for generations. But you may have other, or additional, goals that are equally or more important to you.

Today, many services include reminiscences by friends or family, in addition to any eulogy by the officiant. Family members, friends, and others may speak. Their words often elicit tears, but they may also try the patience of attendees if the speakers drone on. Will you want your family devoting an afternoon to boring any of your friends who bother to show up? Would you rather have beautiful music and a short eulogy by your favorite minister? Would you prefer a celebration of life with a group of friends and family over a buffet lunch and Bloody Mary's? Again, the answers to these questions depend on your preferences and the goals you have for your funeral.

PLANNING YOUR FUNERAL

If you want your funeral to keep building or maintaining your legacy, a well-constructed service and burial are imperative. To that end, you'll want to plan the details of your funeral while you're still able. For instance, a client of great wealth knew exactly what his funeral should look like. He was a patron of the local orchestra and wanted to spotlight its beauty, as both a reflection of their talent and his involvement with the organization.

Working with the conductor many years before his death, he designed a concert with the entire orchestra in mind. At his funeral, the orchestra performed the piece. It was followed by a cocktail reception for the conductor and my client's family. The event was catered by the most expensive restaurant in town. (Rumor has it that the event cost more than his daughter's wedding, which was quite the celebration itself). Everyone had a splendid time. The symphony benefitted from the exposure, and his association with the group was remembered for many years.

Planning must also take into account circumstances that may be beyond your control. For example, Covid disrupted many funerals (including the producer's final act), and spikes and surges in cases may pose similar challenges again. During the height of the pandemic, burials frequently took place with the obituary promising a memorial service or celebration of life after Covid subsided. A friend died in the winter of 2020; his celebration of life was planned outdoors at his favorite charity in the early fall. The invitation stated "Please don't come if you are not vaccinated, and please wear masks. Together we will have cocktails and remember our beloved." That event took a lot of planning by family and others, even including a telephone chain call in the event of rain. Then there have been Zoom funerals and, although there is no enforcement of attendance (who knows who was there), the decedent may be counting heads from above (or below).

If you plan your own funeral before your death, it is critical that everyone knows the details about the service and burial. Without making those details clear to your family, advisors, and support team, your final celebration of life and resting place may not be what you imagined. A relatively young woman, for example, died after a long illness, leaving behind her husband and three grown children. On her deathbed, she called her husband and children together to say she wanted to be cremated. Afterward, her ashes were to be scattered in three locations: the state where she was born, the state where she raised her family, and off the New England coast. She did not include her elderly mother, who was still alive, in those deathbed discussions.

After the woman passed away, her family started planning various ceremonies in line with her last wishes. While doing so, her mother's lawyer called. He explained the woman's grandfather had decreed that every family member was to be buried in the family plot—surrounded by the family's previous five generations—in a graveyard in the town where the family's patriarch had built his business 100 years earlier. The funeral was already arranged and would take place in a small church near the cemetery. The widower and children would have none of it. Their lawyers and the mother's lawyer had to threaten lawsuits and negotiate a settlement, which included a tombstone in the family plot on which some ashes would be dusted. That situation should have been resolved many years earlier, and the woman's involvement during her lifetime would have helped calm the waters and her mother.

This story is not unique. If you have wishes, making your own decisions about your funeral and burial are particularly important. They will help simplify matters for your family as long as you are clear about your plans. By articulating your wishes and making sure everyone involved understands them, you will save your family from difficult choices and potentially awkward discussions.

If you are married, you and your spouse should together

plan your services and final resting places. After all, that spouse will be attending and may have feelings about what would be appropriate. Your decisions might well be based on what will be easiest for your spouse. For example, if your parents and grandparents are all buried in a faraway city, and you plan to be buried in the family plot as well, you should consider how easy it will be for your spouse to visit the grave if you die first, and how your children may feel if that "family plot" has no room for your spouse.

Real complications can develop when there is a second marriage with blended families. Should a widow be buried with her first husband? Where does her second husband then rest? If there are children by both marriages, who decides where one spouse or the other is buried? No matter what you decide, such decisions are best made before the first of you dies, and when you are both fully competent.

A blended family I knew spent a year trying to decide where the father should be buried. The family had not had any discussion on the subject while he was alive. The man's widow had him cremated and kept his ashes in an urn on her fireplace. Meanwhile, her children and his argued over where to scatter them. After patiently waiting for a compromise that would satisfy both families, the widow made a Solomon-like decision. Fortunately, he was a large man with a hefty urn of ashes, so she gave each family half to scatter as they pleased. Incidentally, she remarried a man whose family had a large cemetery plot with plenty of room for her.

YOUR ENDURING LEGACY

What you do during your lifetime is your most lasting legacy, but how you celebrate that lifetime is up to you. Ultimately, obituaries, legacy books and videos, funerals and other services, and burial are your true final stab at legacy. You can design them however you'd like, whether on a yellow legal pad or over a drink by the fire on a chilly night. If you want input from friends and family, you can even design them through a kind of parlor game or other group activity. One fellow I know invited his adult children and wife to a fine dinner with lots of wine. After dinner, he called everyone to another room to help him design his funeral. They spent several hours talking about what he and the family would like to accomplish, who would speak, what music would be played, where he would be buried, and what his tombstone would say. As his son told me many years later, "We had a glorious evening, great wine, and dad thoroughly enjoyed himself."

In addition to your funeral and the like, your final curtain call may include donations to a charitable organization or endowment. For example, one of my clients set up a million-dollar endowment at a hospital to fund healthcare for needy individuals and families. He specified in the deed of gift that, during his lifetime, the fund should be anonymous. After his death, though, he wanted his family name to be associated with the endowment. He told his family that when he died, in lieu of flowers, monetary gifts should be made to that fund as well. His obituary set out the family name of the fund and all memorial gifts went into it. With those, and a substantial gift by various family members, the fund doubled in value. In the process, his name was memorialized much more effectively than if flowers had been sent to his funeral service or scattered gifts had been donated in his name to multiple charities.

Another example can be found in the widow of a professor who had stated in his obituary that gifts should be made to the university and used for purposes he would appreciate, such as scholarships for needy students. Friends, former students, and family contributed $20,000 to that fund. The widow began discussions with the university regarding its use and the administration of the scholarship. She became so engaged in those conversations she gave $500,000 of her own money to a named scholarship program in his honor and folded the memorial contributions into that program.

Interests are developed over your lifetime, not at the time of your death. Make those charitable interests clear and start funding the charity of your choice. By doing so earlier than later, you will have created a vehicle for future gifts. Work on that legacy during your lifetime but allow it to grow bigger once you are gone. Odds and ends of charitable bequests in your will may be nice remembrances. However, creating a program during your lifetime is more likely to encourage others to contribute—and helping others is a lasting legacy indeed.

CONCLUSION

In the end, obituaries, legacy books and videos, and funerals do not *create* legacy. They can enshrine legacy and perpetuate it, but your lifetime deeds, your business and community involvement, and the cherished memories your friends and family have of you, will matter most. Nevertheless, you may reasonably consider the many elements of the final act during your lifetime. You need to share your intentions and thoughts with others who can ensure your wishes are honored. If you decide you'd like to write your own obituary, take time perfecting it, and keep it updated regularly. If you want to write a legacy book or create a video, carefully consider what lessons and messages you want to communicate. And if you are going to plan your own funeral, consider what you want to accomplish. It is important to plan ahead for all of these items, but remember, what's most important is to live life to the fullest. That meticulous producer had it right. The final act and curtain call come only after a fully realized play. It is not the only act in the grand show.

CONCLUSION

A friend's father died at the age of forty-nine. At the time, my friend was still a young man, and it had a profound effect on him. From then on, every morning when he woke up, he'd say a prayer: "Thank you God for giving me another day to get things done." This prayer—and the attitude it reflected in my friend until his death at age seventy-five—encapsulates the spirit every aging wealth holder (every person, in fact) should adopt in youth and embrace over a lifetime. If you wake up every morning grateful for another day to chase your dream and accomplish your goals, life continues to be full.

Still, there are many impediments along the way. As discussed, wealth can be a distraction, rather than a benefit, to continuing your chase and achieving self-actualization. However, wealth can provide some of the support you will need to become all you can be. Realizing that goal—full self-actualization—is as important for the eighty-year-old as it is for the twenty-year-old. To succeed, you need first to define your dream. Then you must build strategies that allow you to continue that chase as you slow down in your later years. Implementing those strategies is not always easy. Indeed, the preceding pages have shown how many challenges you are likely to face as you enter your "golden years."

That's why prioritization and planning are absolutely necessary and must start when you are young. You must give yourself enough time to think clearly about the support you will need, the aspects of your daily life you can either delegate easily or forego altogether, and to explain your wishes and plans to those who will support you. You will need careful and strategic communication with your helping hands, including your partner, children, doctors, and advisors. Over the years, I've had the good fortune of acting as such a helping hand, assisting our clients in finding the right support and navigating those communications. In the process, they discovered that old age can truly be a time when they can continue to be all they can be.

Although talk of funerals, obituaries, and legacies, often comes up in old age, this stage of life should first and foremost be about *living*, feeling part of your world. Aches, pains, and illness make for dull conversation. And if those issues are all you ever focus on, you will have trouble seeing, much less chasing, your dream. You must stay engaged and committed to continuing the chase, waking up every morning with optimism and vigor, regardless of ailments or physical limitations. As you awaken, your aches, pains, and thoughts of last rights should be subsumed in the excitement of what you have to accomplish that day.

We must continue planting the trees for future generations. Like Appius, surround yourself with generations of family if possible; like Churchill, enjoy the liberties of life without the responsibilities that may have bogged down your younger years. Keep your dreams alive and design your old age to give yourself the opportunity to continue the pursuit. That pursuit of self-actualization can lighten the burdens of old age as you continue to chase your dreams.

CONSIDERATION OF ISSUES RELATED TO AGING

SETTING PRIORITIES

Review the list below and rank your top five priorities in order of importance, including subcategories.

EXECUTIVE FUNCTION

- Should assistance be employed if Executive Function impaired?
- Dementia and Alzheimer's
  - Knowledge versus nonrecognition
  - Control versus support
  - Use of "code" word
    - Who should have it?
    - Discussed when and what is word

EMPLOYMENT OF EXPERTS

- Geriatric advisors
- Medical advisors
- Others

HEALTHCARE

- Who decides your approach to healthcare?
- Durable powers of attorney for healthcare
- HIPAA - Who waivers
- "Living Will" Issues
  - Given to doctors?
  - Given to others as needed?
- How to resolve related family disagreements
- Your role if capacity diminished (and how diminished)
- Selection of doctors and second opinions
  - Medical decisions
  - Experts to determine competency

RESIDENCE

- Expression of desire
  - Living alone
  - Assisted living
  - 24-hour caregivers
- Companionship
- Maintaining residence
  - Who is responsible for maintaining your home?
  - Condition desired, including improvements, cleanliness, wear and tear
  - Improvements required for independent living
    - To what extent and what cost before you consider assisted living?
- Geography
  - Staying "put" or moving near children
- Maintaining for "two" if partnered

PARTNERS

- Desired or not
- Financial support of partner
- Condition of partner and assuming responsibility for him or her

DRIVING

- Test regularly
- Willingness to have car taken away by others. If so, who is in charge of that task?
- Thoughts with respect to alternatives

TRAVEL

- Should that be encouraged/ discouraged?
  - ° Who balances cost vs. benefits?

LEGACY AND RELEVANCE

- Boards and other community roles
  - ° What to do if not capable to perform duties
  - ° Should family take action or leave it to organization?
- Employment
  - ° Assistance from support staff
- Responsibility for dependent employees
  - ° Should those be assumed by others?

COLLECTIBLES AND TANGIBLES

- Who takes over management and disposition?
  - ° What actions are you willing to have taken during your lifetime?
  - ° Disposition on "downsizing" residence?

MEMBERSHIPS

- Should they be maintained?
- Religious affiliations/congregations
- Social Clubs
- Country Clubs/Lunch Clubs
- Health Clubs
- Other memberships

WISHES FOR BURIAL, FUNERAL, DONATION, AND OBITUARY

- Funeral purpose
- Who writes obituary?
  ° What charity and when?
- Whether and where to be buried
- Building charitable legacy

CHARLES A. LOWENHAUPT is a recognized leader and wealth counselor for ultra-high net worth individuals and families around the world. He is Chairman and Partner of Lowenhaupt & Chasnoff, LLC, the first U.S. law firm to concentrate in tax law and established by Charles' grandfather in 1908. Charles is also Global Chairman of Lowenhaupt Global Advisors Australia, a family office based in Sydney.

Charles is a Founding Advisory Faculty member of the Institute for Private Investors. He is also a co-founder of the Leadership Center for Investment Stewards, President of the St. Louis Art Museum Subdistrict Commission, and a Director of the Urban League of Metropolitan St. Louis and of the American Jewish Joint Distribution Committee. He also was President of Temple Emanuel in St. Louis (2010-2012) and is a former Member of the St. Louis Zoo Subdistrict (1989 – 1992) and a former director of Clements Library of the University of Michigan in Ann Arbor (1997-2014). Charles has a Bachelor of Arts degree (cum laude) from Harvard University. He also has a Juris Doctorate (Order of the Coif) from the University of Michigan Law School. He is a member of the Bar of Missouri and New York. Charles is the author of two books: *Freedom from Wealth* (with Don Trone) and *The Wise Inheritor's Guide to Freedom from Wealth*. In 2019, *Family Wealth Report* awarded Charles its Thought Leadership award for his contributions to the wealth management industry. In 2011, *Private Asset Management* named Charles one of the 25 most influential people in wealth management and family office services.

ENDNOTES

1 Marcus Tullius Cicero, "Cato Maior de Senectute," ed. E. S. Shuckburgh, *Tulli Ciceronis: Cato Maior de Senectute*, London: Macmillan Co., 1895, http://www.forumromanum.org/literature/cicero/sen.html#38.

2 Alzheimer's Association, "Alzheimer's and Dementia: Facts and Figures," 2021, https://www.alz.org/alzheimers-dementia/facts-figures.

3 Marina Bolotnikova, "America's car crash epidemic," *Vox*, September 19, 2021, https://www.vox.com/22675358/us-car-deaths-year-traffic-covid-pandemic.

4 Carol Pogash, "Asian Art Museum to Remove Bost of Patron. That's Just a Start." *The New York Times*, June 15, 2020, https://www.nytimes.com/2020/06/15/arts/design/avery-brundage-bust-asian-art-museum.html.

www.ingramcontent.com/pod-product-compliance
Lightning Source LLC
Chambersburg PA
CBHW031503180326
41458CB00044B/6671/J